ernst barlach

ernst barlach

BY ALFRED WERNER

McGraw-Hill Book Company · New York · London · Toronto · Sydney

ERNST BARLACH

Library of Congress Catalog Card Number: 66–16774

69440

To Judith

Contents

ernst barlach

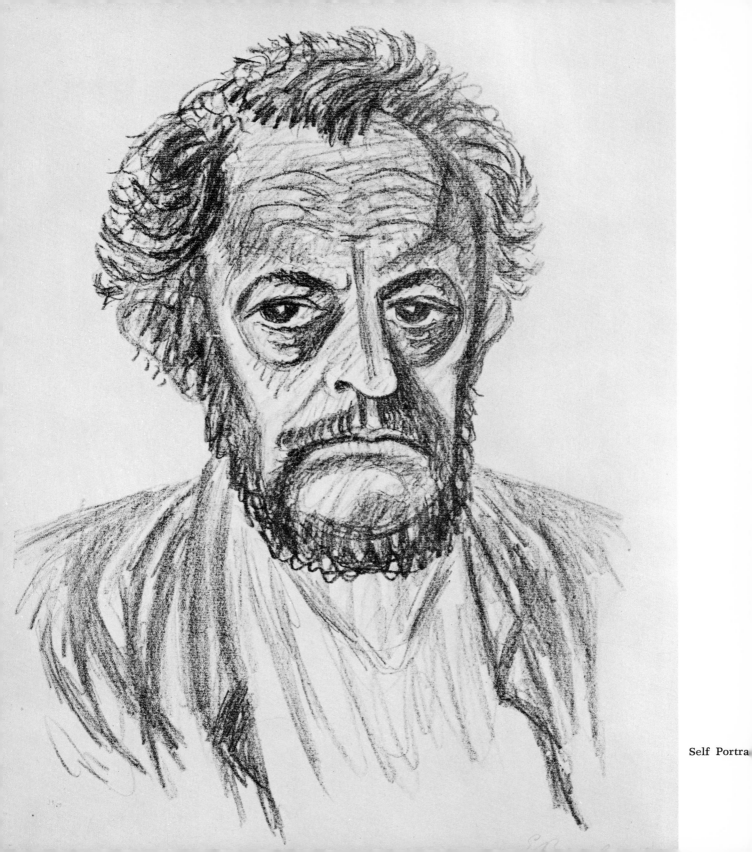

Self Portra

I consider Barlach one of the greatest sculptors we Germans have had.

Bertolt Brecht

Talented men are not rare in any period, any land. Rare, however, are men like Ernst Barlach (1870–1938) who possess wisdom in addition to the manual skill and fantasy that are the qualifications of every good artist.

Ernst Barlach was as kind to his fellow men as he was wise, yet unbending where his principles were at stake. His devotion to truth was tempered by a sense of proportion and a pervasive humor. Sculptor, printmaker, poet, he inspired more love and respect than any other artist active in Central Europe in the early decades of this century. Flaubert admonished the young de Maupassant that a man who has set himself up to be an artist no longer has a right to live like other people, that he has to consider life as a means and nothing more, and that the first person he should disregard is himself. Barlach would have agreed wholeheartedly. By his very manner of living, he proved—if any proof is necessary—the fallacy of narcissism and hedonism that so often has marred the creativeness of unusual men.

Barlach, who whimsically liked to call himself a "barbarian," deviated from the popular image of the artist by being an extraordinarily well-read, well-informed man. The literature, philosophy,

3

music and, of course, plastic art of various periods and nations engaged his attention, and in his voluminous writings there are allusions to Carlyle and Nietzsche, Goethe, Dostoevski and even Li Po, to Bach and Beethoven, and to Michelangelo and Gruene-wald, Rembrandt and Daumier. Thus he, a decidedly Germanic figure, rooted in the moral and aesthetic traditions and the harsh strength of Protestant Northern Germany, was a man at home in the supranational realm where all the great can meet.

Still, in a sense, he was an isolated phenomenon even in his own country. While his name is often mentioned in connection with the Expressionists, the differences are perhaps greater than the affinities.[1] The men of the *Bruecke,* and even more those of the *Blauer Reiter,* had links with revolutionary artists elsewhere, especially those in France, even though they might have had reservations about their French colleagues. These men threw themselves intensely into the intellectual struggles of Berlin, drew inspiration from its night life and social conflicts, and were often harshly critical of what they found there. In varying degrees they were active in politics, and for a time nearly all were affiliated with the *Novembergruppe,* which sought a close alliance between creative men and the newly born German Republic. In their work they were freer, looser, more informal than Barlach—and are therefore more attractive to the post-World War II generation, which is often blind to the aesthetic and ethical values represented by Barlach (or by his friend, Kaethe Kollwitz).[2]

Compared to most of his German contemporaries, Barlach was a provincial recluse. As much as he could, he avoided Berlin, where the majority of his colleagues lived at one time or another. His days were spent chiefly in small and obscure German towns. He did not have the wanderlust that drove Nolde and Pechstein to the South Seas, Macke and Klee to North Africa, though he once did visit Southern Russia. On his two sojourns in France he did not, like Wilhelm Lehmbruck, seek out the rebellious men of the *École de Paris,* but remained in the company of other German artists. He spent some months in Italy, but felt happier when he again had German soil under his feet. Retrospectively he even made the astonishing statement that he considered Guestrow (the tiny and drab town in Mecklenburg where he settled for good) equal to any city in Tuscany.

He had few intimate friends among artists and writers, and those few were, with one or two exceptions, minor figures. He had no close connection to any political party, though he was attracted to Socialism, or rather to a kind of ideal, utopian Communism that had little resemblance to the system that was to develop in Russia. While he was aware of the vigorous new movements in art, he flatly rejected the tenets of Kandinsky and candidly admitted that he had "no eye" for Picasso. Except for traces of the *Jugendstil* of 1900 (the *Art Nouveau* of Germany) to be seen in his early work, he did not allow any contemporary style to influence him. Expressionism is indebted to him for stimuli, and not the other way around. He had not even the most tenuous links to the Expressionist groups, and his name is absent from all Expressionist manifestoes. He was more profoundly influenced by the saints carved in wood by pre-Renaissance German craftsmen than by any sculpture of his own day. Philosophically he felt closer to the mysticism of Old Russia, and to Buddhism, than to the ideologies that prevailed at the turn of the century and thereafter.

Yet with all his limitations—self-limitations might be a more precise term—to those who know the totality of his work he appears a figure as powerful and many-sided as Michelangelo. Indeed, Barlach might be viewed as a provincial Michelangelo of the Low German lands. Both had exceptional gifts in many areas of artistic activity, both worked ceaselessly and unselfishly to achieve perfection, both put up a heroic resistance to any compromise, both were devoid of social graces, lonely men, for the better part of their lives, both had to endure vexations of all sorts. Frustrated, hampered in many ways, Michelangelo wrote, "I am stoned every day as if I had crucified Christ." Barlach's letters too are full of justifiably bitter complaints. But the similarity is not only biographical. In passion as well as depth of introspection (and even in his ascetic features) the versatile Barlach resembled the *uomo universale,* whose monuments in the Medici Chapel made a lasting impression upon him. Barlach once observed that it was his aim to present not what he saw, but *"das Wirkliche und Wahrhaftige,"* the real and the true. Michelangelo could have said this of himself; in fact his poems do say much the same thing.

Both men were carvers who chose refractory media—Michelangelo, marble; Barlach, the less resistant wood—and freed the intended form from the enclosing block by cutting away all irrelevant matter, always with reverence for the unique and distinctive qualities of the material. Their lives were dedicated to the search for ultimate solutions, artistic as well as metaphysical, to link the inner world with the outer, to explore the bottomless depth beneath the surface of reality, to reveal through the senses the wellsprings of the soul. Both needed man's body, man's face, to make their most stirring statements. What Georg Brandes wrote about Michelangelo might also be applied to the master born four centuries later: "He soon discovered that he could say all he wanted to say by means of the human body. . . . It alone was his theme and his work, his means and his end."

But while Michelangelo needed the courts of the Pope and the Medici, Barlach chose to retreat to a small town where another man might have perished from boredom. He found all the subjects he required in the simple, dour folk of Holstein and Mecklenburg, in the farmers, fishermen and tradespeople of the Lower Elbe region and the Baltic hinterland. Quiet, even phlegmatic, and endowed with a weird humor, they served as models for the figures he drew on paper, carved into wood, or transmuted into the characters of the plays he wrote. Hence, for an understanding of Barlach it may help to have visited the vast stretches of flat, austere, rain- and fog-ridden land washed by many rivers and lakes, a German steppe where the winters are severe, where spooks and phantoms abound. It may be enlightening to have

6

seen Barlach's uncelebrated towns, with their plain old brick churches filled with carvings by 15th-century Barlachs.

Yet it would be a mistake to think of his work as regional. Although Barlach once wrote that he was pleased to have been called a "plattdeutscher Bildhauer," a Low German sculptor, he did not confine himself to plastic expression of the features of his rustic neighbors, and he certainly did not content himself with portraying what Berliners would cherish as primitive and quaint. Ordinary naturalism, Barlach knew, cannot pierce the masks worn by man, and what mattered to him was the hidden essence rather than the obvious details.

True, he paid much attention to the world of everyday. But even the sketches which, at twenty-five, he made in the streets of Paris appeared to his French host, himself an artist, "*très philosophiques*." As he grew older, he set himself ever higher goals. The Russians, whom he had seen briefly, and the Holsteiners and Mecklenburgers, among whom he lived regularly, were transformed into vessels into which he poured his own life. He endowed them with his own soul—that of a haunted, damned, bewitched being, shaken by fate, yet still undaunted, aware as he was of his origin in what, for lack of a better word, might be called God.[3] It was the soul of one who had the strength to endure physical as well as spiritual pain, one who, though not affiliated with any church, possessed that true religiosity which can carry us into the sphere of calm, serene contemplation, where sorrows are no longer vexations but have become guiding lights.

This does much to explain why Barlach's influence has spread far beyond the boundaries of his native country. He has been discovered in Scandinavia, Switzerland, Holland, England, Italy, and the United States. Nor is the fact that Barlach turned his back to the abstract revolution a reason why his idiom should be less comprehensible to his spiritual grandchildren. For the basic terms and the basic grammar have not changed, and the best in the art of the past is timelessly "abstract" in the sense of transcending the material, of stressing the archetypal rather than

7

the ordinary. Barlach tried to give concrete form to something entirely abstract—man's soul. As he wrote in his autobiography: "A mighty realization burst upon me, and this is what it was: To you it is given to express, without reserve, all that is within you —the uttermost, the innermost, the gentle gesture of piety and the rude gesture of rage—because for everything, be it paradise, hell, or one in the guise of the other, there is expressive form."

His work lives. It illuminates all the heights and depths of human existence, turns stark dissonances into harmony. What touches us in it most profoundly is the supreme individuality of the mind that has created it. In all his work Barlach's severe face appears—the countenance of a struggling man.

Paul Schurek, Barlach's friend and biographer

The market town of Wedel, Holstein, is on the right bank of the slow, broad, majestic Elbe, some miles west of Hamburg, on a marshy plain protected by dykes. Once it was a member of the Hanseatic League, but by the 19th century it had lost all of its former importance. Today Wedel consists of what the devastations of the Second World War have spared of the historic center, with its low gabled houses and the medieval statue of Roland, and a sprawling new section, with modern homes, schools, offices and shops. The large but unadorned house in the old quarter where Ernst Barlach was born on January 2, 1870 now bears a simple commemorative plaque.[4] His paternal grandfather was a Protestant pastor. His father, Dr. Georg Barlach, was a general practitioner whose patients were scattered throughout the rural district. Dr. Barlach's wife Louise, the daughter of a customs inspector named Vollert, gave birth to four sons, of whom only Ernst, the oldest, was to make a name for himself. Every member of his father's family seems to have drawn or painted for recreation. Hence Barlach writes, almost with a sigh of relief, that his mother "neither painted nor drew."

Ernst was not a precocious child like Albrecht Duerer, who was an accomplished artist by thirteen. Occasionally Ernst modeled clay birds for his own and his playmates' amusement, but the results were no more promising than was his early verse. He found it difficult to draw, not for lack of talent, but possibly because in his naiveté he was too eager to reproduce accurately the illustrations for a certain edition of Hauff's *Maerchen* which he owned. He had yet a long way to go to discover the merits of spontaneity. Still he considered one of his drawings good enough to give to his father for Christmas. Dr. Barlach hung it in his office. *"Det hett min Jung makt"* (my boy did that) he explained to a patient. The simple peasant replied in the same Low German dialect, *"Det muett jo een kloken Jung sein"* (he must be a clever boy).

Ernst was not only a "clever boy," he was also a healthy and happy child who roamed the still unspoiled neighborhood with his three brothers, who were only slightly younger, and he was not averse to pranks à la Till Eulenspiegel. Dr. Barlach took his oldest son along in his open carriage as he made his rounds, and related to him whatever he remembered of the Greek myths. On these trips, too, the boy had his first encounters with sickness, suffering and even death. (In Norway's capital city, Christian Munch, M.D. took his son Edvard to the slums, believing that children should become acquainted with the tragic aspects of life.) Dr. Barlach was a most conscientious physician. One night the coach was not available. Though he himself was sick, he walked a long distance in response to an emergency call. The resulting pneumonia led to his death at the age of forty-five. The widow's health was far from steady; she had just recovered from a lengthy spell of mental illness. Nonetheless she carried as well as she could the responsibility of rearing her sons in a household where money was scarce. Ernst was sent to study in the secondary schools of Ratzeburg and Schoenberg, small towns further east to which the Barlachs had successively moved. He left school when he was eighteen, without undergoing the final examinations.

Ernst was not unduly concerned that he had not received the

diploma (*Reifezeugnis*) required for study at a university, for he knew that he wanted to become an artist. To eke out a livelihood, he decided to become a *Zeichenlehrer* (teacher of drawing), and with this in mind, he enrolled in 1888 at the *Kunstgewerbeschule* (School of Applied Arts) in Hamburg. His teacher, himself a pupil of the Danish sculptor, Albert Bertel Thorvaldsen, whose highly accomplished, coldly intellectual imitations of Greek sculpture have since fallen out of favor, saw the young man's sketches and recommended that he abandon his efforts because he would never produce anything worthwhile.

Barlach refused to accept this verdict. From 1891 to 1895 he studied at the Academy of Art in Dresden, where his abilities were more readily acknowledged. In May 1895, after having gone through this mill of rigid and largely unimaginative instruction, he journeyed to Paris with a friend, Carl Garbers. For a while he studied at the Académie Julian, but eventually he rebelled against the method of teaching that limited him to overly precise drawing of the nude model. He came to loathe those "miserable, monotonous accuracies, states of a miserable, monotonous nakedness of male and female, offerings lacking in consolation." Once he was out again on the street and free to sketch everything he saw in the fascinating city, the pencil in his hand "began to dance with impatience." [5] Later he was to remark that whatever he had learned he had received from the streets rather than from academies or museums.

He did go to the Louvre, and he was profoundly impressed, particularly by its treasures of Egyptian art. But he seems to have paid little attention to the French artists of the day. Neither in his autobiography nor in his Parisian sketches is there any mention of the two outstanding events of 1895: the Monet exhibition at Durand-Ruel's and the Cézanne show at Vollard's. What little he may have seen of Rodin's work does not appear to have impressed him. [6] There is no evidence that as a young man he saw any works by Daumier, whom he was later to admire. It may be assumed that young Barlach did not care too much for French art, and that he overrated certain German academicians whose work has now fallen into oblivion.

To keep the wolf from his door, occasionally Barlach drew sketches for *Die fliegenden Blaetter*, a somewhat low-brow satirical weekly. (Later the far superior *Jugend* and *Simplicissimus*, also weeklies, were to publish his sometimes humorous and sometimes bitterly ironic cartoons.) He and his friend Garbers also accepted a commission to carve for the Rathskeller in Hamburg a statue of Hebe, cupbearer to the Gods. The fees were small, but the two did not allow the limitation of funds to spoil the pleasures of Bohemian life. From this period a self-portrait of Barlach survives; the oil shows him as a romantic student, with a reddish-blond Henri-Quatre beard and dressed in the usual attire of an artist in Montmartre.

Barlach returned to Germany in the spring of 1896 without having profited much from his stay abroad. He mailed his paint-box to his cousin Karl, having decided that oils were not his medium. In 1897 there was a second interlude in Paris to assist Garbers in the execution of another commission. From his twenty-sixth to his thirty-sixth year he worked furiously both as a writer and as a sculptor, but the period was one of indecision and anxiety, of frustration and despair rather than of fulfillment and success. For seven months he taught at a trade school of ceramics in Hoehr, in the hills of Westerwald, where most of Germany's beer mugs come from. But he gave it up because he disliked teaching (although to judge by the textbook for figure drawing which he published and which went through several editions, he had a distinct talent for pedagogy). In addition to drawing for magazines, he collaborated on a large figure of Neptune commissioned by the Hamburg-American Shipping Line. For his daily bread he also modeled small figures in clay which were cast in a ceramic factory; designed bronze plaques, and did other commercial work which later in life he did not consider worthwhile. He was to write: "Everything that I produced before the age of thirty-six [before 1907] I can dismiss easily." Undoubtedly Barlach's judgment of himself was too severe. In

1902 Karl Scheffler, a leading critic, in his magazine, *Die Kunst fuer Alle*, published an analysis of Barlach's work and, while noting that the artist was still groping for an adequate manner of expression, found much to praise. In the same year, one of Barlach's bronze plaques was chosen for the International Exhibition of Applied Arts at Turin, Italy.

Personal difficulties developed. A heart ailment, which had made itself felt in Paris, now returned; fortunately, it responded to medical treatment. There was also trouble of another nature. A liaison with a woman whom he did not wish to marry presented him with the prospect of a child born out of wedlock. To forget his problems for a while, he was only too happy to accompany his brother Nikolaus on a journey to Kharkov in the Ukraine, where their brother Hans was prospering as an engineer. This journey—August 2 to September 27, 1906—in a sense became for Barlach what the hegira was for Mohammed. In the Ukraine, Barlach found the manner of expression he had desired. He had penetrated beneath the surface:

"I found in Russia this amazing unity of inward and outward being, this symbolic quality: this is what we human beings are, at bottom all beggars and problem characters (*problematische Existenzen*). . . . It shines out of the Slav, while others hide it."

Perhaps he was to feel later on that too much importance had been attached by critics to this Russian experience, that they were wrong in thinking that in Russia the ultimate plastic solution had fallen, so to speak, into his lap: "Really and truly I am not without a share in the essence of the final outcome." Yet on the steppe Barlach seems to have had visions similar to those of a slightly earlier traveler, the poet Rainer Maria Rilke, who wrote that Russia had given him the words for those religious depths of his nature that had striven for expression since his childhood. The immediate fruits of Barlach's trips were sketches of peasants, pencil drawings which in their stark melancholy are reminiscent of those young Vincent van Gogh made at Nuenen. His *Doppelbegabung* (double gift) also allowed him to relate with the vividness of a poet all he saw:

". . . Peasants in extraordinary coats, garments of strangely uniform antediluvian shapes, one could almost say cut pachyderm fashion . . . the skinny exterior broken up and falling into folds and creases, draped one way or another so as ruthlessly to cover up all anatomical subtleties and different ways of motion, and thereby to evoke a simplified human type."

These short, squat, round-headed, slit-eyed, flat-faced beggars, monks, pilgrims and peasant women on the steppe were indeed "sitting bronzes," as he visualized them, anticipating his future cast of characters: moujiks, with Slavic high cheekbones, primitive people untouched by any veneer of civilization, monumental in their immobility, set against the immensity of the plains, always waiting, but not knowing for whom or for what. More important, however, than the subject matter Barlach brought back was the new and higher metaphysics to which these experiences led him. Many miles away from contemporary materialism and rationalism, he felt he had observed in a capsule form all the misery of the human race and its ardent desire for salvation.

In 1909 he made his last major journey abroad. A traveling fellowship gave him ten carefree months at the Villa Romana in Florence. He was thrilled by the landscape, and he was impressed by whatever remnants of the art of the ancient Etruscans he saw, but on the whole he was not deeply influenced. "Italy," he summed up, "would have bowled me over had I been a painter which, fortunately, I was not." It is significant that at the site of so many celebrated monuments in marble he continued to work in wood (a medium he had begun with two years earlier) and in the anti-classical manner which, since the Russian adventure, he had made his own. One of the benefits derived from his Italian stay was his lifelong friendship with the ecstatic poet Theodor Daeubler, like Barlach a German Expressionist with much to separate him from the Expressionist school. Daeubler was the first German literary man to write enthusiastically about Barlach, still relatively unappreciated in his native country. Daeubler's remarkable Jupiter head and enormous rotund phy-

1. Russian Beggar Woman
Russische Bettlerin
Ceramic

2. The Melon Eater
Der Melonenesser
Bronze

sique inspired Barlach to several portraits in different media. Daeubler also appears, undisguised, in Barlach's unfinished novel, *Seespeck*.

In 1910 Barlach, with his mother and his four-year-old son, moved to Guestrow where his brother Joseph had set up a business selling agricultural machinery. This town of less than twenty thousand in the grand duchy of Mecklenburg-Schwerin was better known for its cattle shows than for any cultural activities.[7] Yet it was quiet, and he needed quiet to work "like a medieval craftsman." The man who enabled him to live for his work alone was Berlin's avant-garde dealer, the enterprising and astute Paul Cassirer, who had spotted two of his terra cottas at a group show staged in Berlin by the artists' association, *Sezession,* to which Barlach belonged. Cassirer quickly reached an agreement with the unworldly and impractical man, still little known: for a modest yet sufficient income, Barlach was to turn over all the work he produced. Thus he could concentrate entirely on his creative efforts. The arrangement was to work out satisfactorily for both parties over the years without friction.

There were to be interruptions for Barlach, though. A pleasant one was the short trip to Holland the artist undertook in 1912 in the company of his dealer and the latter's wife, the actress Tilla Durieux: now he had a chance to study the masterworks of Rembrandt in Amsterdam and The Hague, and those of Frans Hals in Haarlem. Two years later the war broke out. At first Barlach—like so many German intellectuals, Thomas Mann included—firmly believed the cause of the Central Powers to be a just one. In his diaries he cheerfully listed each German victory. Gradually, however, his enthusiasm waned, until by 1916 he was convinced that a German defeat was inevitable; moreover, he had become "*kriegsmuede*" (war weary) long before the fighting was over. Though he contributed a few lithographs to publications dedicated to the war effort, none stooped to glorify the great destruction of lives, and some were even outright "defeatist."[8] Barlach confessed he had little "*Hasskraft*" (faculty for hating).

He himself, being forty-four at the start of the war, was at first left alone by the authorities, and to contribute his share served as a volunteer helper in a day center for soldiers' children whose mothers had to work. Finally the recruiting officers caught up with him and dispatched him to a training camp for the army reserve in North Schleswig where the unsoldierly thinker and dreamer cut a sorry figure. Fortunately, he was returned to civilian life after ten harassing weeks.[9]

After lengthy litigation he had obtained custody of Nikolaus, whom he had legitimized, giving him his name. Now, he had to devote a good deal of time to the upbringing and education of his son, whose grandmother was growing older and weaker. The twenties began for Barlach with a personal tragedy. Frau Barlach, who had been sent to a mental hospital, managed to commit suicide by drowning herself in a nearby lake. Shaken by the catastrophe, the artist found solace in his work and in his growing reputation. He had been able to exchange his original studio in an erstwhile potter's shed for a larger place that had formerly served as a stable. But he had to wait until he was sixty to be able to build himself, just outside the town in a pine grove, a really spacious studio equipped with all he needed for his work.

He was sixty when the flood of incoming congratulatory messages finally convinced his fellow-townsmen that he was an outstanding person and made them proud of his presence among them. For years they had treated him with suspicion, as the townfolk of Nuenen or Arles had resented Van Gogh. Unlike Vincent, Barlach refrained from any conduct that the most conservative burgher could object to. But the townsmen felt that his profession was reason enough for being wary of him. Besides, if he amounted to anything, they reasoned, he surely would be living in Berlin rather than remaining in their little town.

To make things more difficult Barlach was indeed a strange sight. Totally unconcerned about his appearance, a slight man with an ascetic face surrounded by an unruly beard, with large, unforgettably sad eyes above dark, hollow pouches, and with a melancholy, severe mouth, he looked completely different from the plain, flat Guestrowers whom we see in his drawings, sculptures and prints. His thin form wrapped in an old brown cloak that badly needed mending appeared to the citizens like a phantom from another world. It was as if a saint painted by El Greco had come to life, to descend upon a dryly rational town in Mecklenburg.

People knew and respected him in the large cities, however, especially in Berlin, where Cassirer had given him a comprehensive one-man show in 1917. When in the following year the Kaiserreich collapsed, Barlach was forty-eight. Under the Weimar Republic, honors that were long overdue were heaped upon him. In 1919 he was made a member of the Academy of Arts in Berlin and in 1925, of the Academy in Munich. Berlin and Dresden offered him professorships, but he wanted to continue to create rather than to teach. In 1924 one of his plays, *Die Suendflut* (The Flood) was awarded the much-coveted Kleist Prize, named for an important 19th-century German dramatist. Several of his plays were produced, but he saw only one performance—Leopold Jessner's production of *Die echten Sedemunds* (The Genuine Sedemunds) at the Berlin State Theater—or rather part of it, for he walked out after the first act, horrified by the "fantastic, unnatural marionette style" of the staging since, as he put it, he had written about "real people."

By 1930 he had become one of Germany's most famous artists, and his reputation had spread as far as the United States. In that year his sixtieth birthday was celebrated all over Germany. His sculptures in wood were exhibited at the Academy in Berlin. The show was opened with a speech by the octogenarian Max Liebermann, the Academy's honorary president, but without Barlach putting in an appearance—there was, as he put it, "too little curiosity" in him. He did go to Berlin, though, to view his bronzes —his new dealer Alfred Flechtheim had gotten his consent to the casting in bronze of some of his preliminary sketches in clay. At the opening a meeting between the sculptor and his French colleague, Aristide Maillol, was arranged. No two more dissimilar sculptors could have met. Maillol was a pagan sensualist who

3. Russian Beggar Woman
Russische Bettlerin
Ceramic

stressed the solidity of the flesh and the gentle firmness of a woman's curves; he created a nude universe in which there was neither sin nor remorse, neither the heart's anguish nor the body's decay. *"Tu es Nordique—moi, je suis Méditerranée,"* Maillol said to Barlach with a smile that emphasized the contrast.

Since Barlach shunned openings as well as the artists' cafés of the capital, many people eager to shake his hand and to express their admiration made the long trip to remote Guestrow to see the man around whom a veil of myths had already descended. But he wanted to be left alone, to work in peace:

"Barlach would go to hide himself around the time the train from Berlin came in," his friend, Kaethe Kollwitz, recalled. "He would peep out, and if there were any people pacing back and forth before his house in a suspicious fashion, he would duck back into his hiding place until the visitors had left."

He was basically shy. Besides, he had no minutes to spare, for there were many commissions to execute. His earliest war memorial—a wood relief of a sword-pierced *Mater Dolorosa*— was done for the Nikolai Church of Kiel. Then came the memorial for the cathedral in Guestrow, a solemn large bronze angel with a mystic, disembodied look and with features resembling Frau Kollwitz; suspended from the ceiling above a tablet, it commemorated the fallen soldiers. The third work in this category was another large bronze, the *Geistkaempfer* (Champion of the Spirit), a tall slim angel brandishing a sword and standing upon a rapacious beast representing evil. This group was placed in front of the University Church in Kiel. The cathedral of Magdeburg acquired an *Ehrenmal* (memorial) in wood: three standing soldiers and, below them, a helmeted Death flanked by a veiled mourning woman and a man with a gas mask on his chest. To commemorate Hamburg's victims of war he made, on a huge limestone shaft, an intaglio carving of a widow and her daughter.

Of a different nature was the *Gemeinschaft der Heiligen* (Community of Holy Ones). To fill sixteen empty niches on the façade of an unused Gothic church at Luebeck, Carl Georg Heise, superintendent of fine arts, urged Barlach to make symbolic stone figures; only three were finished by the artist at the time the Nazis came to power, and both Heise and Barlach, his protégé, had become *personae non gratae*. Among the private commissions were a Beethoven frieze, parts of which were subsequently used for a series entitled *Fries der Lauschenden* (Frieze of Listeners), and important grave monuments.

But even the twenties were not a period of uninterrupted bliss for a man with the character and convictions of Barlach. It is too easily forgotten that Nazism did not arise abruptly in March 1933. Like Thomas Mann he had become a staunch pacifist, and one of the few friends the Weimar Republic could boast of. All of his war memorials were bitterly attacked by the Right Wing as defeatist since he failed to portray a strong Teutonic youth in a steel helmet, throwing a hand grenade. Unknown extremists even tried to mutilate one of them.[10] The town of Malchin in Pomerania first ordered from him a war memorial—and then reversed its decision, after some of the city fathers had denounced him as a Jew, and a Communist sympathizer.[11]

Barlach did not consider it an insult to be called a Jew; while anti-Semitism was endemic in many Germans, Barlach was utterly free of it. When berated for having "sold himself to that Jew Cassirer," the artist sternly retorted, "I wish that all Christian dealers were as generous and honest as he." Barlach was on friendly terms with several Jewish intellectuals; he was appreciative of the devotion of Berlin's Jewish collectors who gave his works places of honor in their homes, and he was to continue cordial correspondence with his Jewish friends and acquaintances after they had been forced to emigrate, despite the fact that the Nazis were watching his mail. He belonged to no political party, yet he once, by his own admission, voted for the *Deutsche Demokratische Partei* led by Walther Rathenau, who was a target and finally a victim of the nationalists. He read with interest Leopold Schwarzschild's *Tagebuch*, a pacifist weekly, slightly left-of-center, to which he once contributed a brief essay. Altogether he was an independent man, who, on the few occasions that he gave vent to his political convictions, did so without shrinking from the wrath of the extremists on the left or on the right.

Having been insulted by proto-Nazis and Nazis long before the disintegration of democracy in Germany, he had no illusions about his adversaries.[12] As early as December 1930 he wrote to a friend, "All these people, Nazis and Stahlhelmers [the *Stahlhelm* was a militaristic organization] are instinctively my enemies, evil wishers from the unaccountable flow of their very blood; they will make short shrift of me when the hour comes." Prophetic words, as were these: "I fear all this inflamed younger generation will have to be chastised with scorpions before they learn to see things differently."

He was more clairvoyant politically than most of his friends, who believed that the Nazis would never come to power, that common sense would prevail. On the other hand, he was sufficiently naïve to think that he could fight Hitlerism single-handed by writing articles for the anti-Nazi press: it was outlawed before the ink on his paper had dried. Still he deserves our profound respect for being different from those who out of sheer "prudence" refrained from making any move. Hitler was definitely on the threshold on January 23, 1933, when Barlach delivered an address over the German radio which left no doubt as to his stand. Ostensibly *Der Kuenstler und seine Zeit* ("The Artist and His Time") was no political utterance, and Barlach did avoid naming any particular party. But the voice of the recluse from Guestrow was clearly brimming with indignation over the Nazi threat to freedom. The gist of the speech was a warning against blind acceptance of any dogma, religious, national or economic, and a plea to reject any panacea that had not proven its worth under close scrutiny.

A week later Adolf Hitler was appointed Chancellor of the Reich.

One old peasant with bowed back was heard to remark that after the Guestrow monument had been taken away his soul couldn't rest any more—he didn't know where the angel had gone.

From a UP report, 1938

Nothing would have pleased Barlach more than to live out his years in peace without becoming a center of controversy, and without the loud publicity that marked him simultaneously a "cultural Bolshevist" at home and a "victim of Fascism" abroad. The mistreatment of Barlach by Hitler's minions is one of the darkest episodes in the thousand-year conflict of the creative personality with aesthetically limited authorities. For while the rejection of an artist is defensible,[13] it is criminal to stifle him because he will not yield an inch from his position, as was the case with the unshakeable Barlach. While he was not sent to a concentration camp and was allowed to die of "natural causes," he was, in his own words, forced to lead the life of an emigrant in his own native land and was finally "garrotted." There can be no doubt that the constant vexations to which his sick heart was subjected hastened his end.

It is odd that as late as February 1933 he received the first and only honor to be given him by the Reich: he was made a Knight of the Order *Pour le Mérite*.[14] Among those who had cast their ballots for him were two aged friends, Max Liebermann and Kaethe Kollwitz, and the award was presented to him by the

4. Beggar Woman with Child
Bettlerin mit Kind
Plaster

5. Seated Peasant Woman
Sitzende Baeuerin
Porcelain

famous physicist, Max von Planck, also an old-fashioned liberal. But this was just a holdover from the Weimar Republic. A few weeks later, with Hitler having been voted into power, the distinction would certainly not have gone to one who in his public monuments had "slapped the national consciousness in the face."

Barlach was legitimately represented in the large exhibition, *Arte e Resistenza in Europa*, that was seen in two Italian cities in 1965. For while a good many of the German artists went to great lengths to ingratiate themselves with the very men who had humiliated them and ostracized their work, Barlach belonged to the bold minority who maintained a defiant dignity when attacked as "degenerates." [15] He even wrote to the President of the Academy of Arts, the composer Max von Schillings, express-

6. Russian Lovers
Russisches Liebespaar
Porcelain

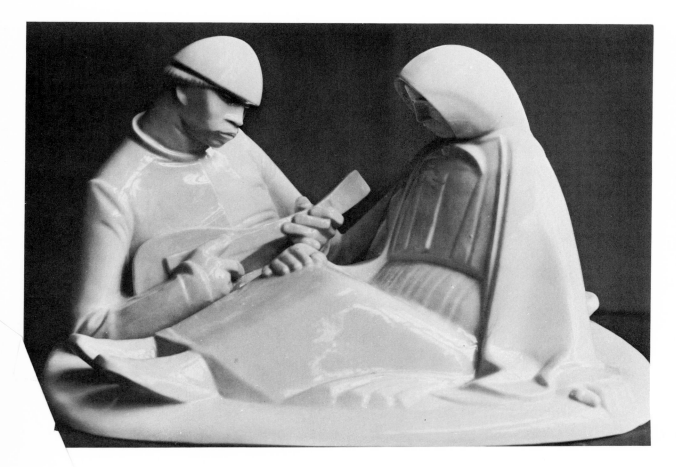

ing his concern about the "voluntary" withdrawal from Academy membership by Kollwitz and Liebermann. To Goebbels he protested against the treatment of his work in a letter that left no doubt about his own opposition to Nazism.[16] To the Nazi *Reichsstatthalter* (governor) of Mecklenburg, for whom Barlach was "*volksfremd*" (without roots in the national German character), and who had coldly advised the artist to emigrate, he explained proudly:

"I have lived in Mecklenburg for thirty years . . . there is scarcely a person in all Germany who has, from the very beginning, derived more of the form and essence of his work from his close ties with the German nation. . . . I am so deeply rooted in this country that the thought of leaving, of seeking my fortunes as an emigrant, is very far from my mind. I shall stay at my post whatever the consequences."

But neither Goebbels nor the governor replied to the artist's firm plea to stop what he characterized as "despicable" actions. With the exception of the *Mater Dolorosa* in Kiel, which somehow was overlooked, his war memorials were removed one after another.[17] It must be admitted that the Nazi hierarchy was not unanimous in the condemnation of Barlach's art. Goebbels is said to have owned some of his works, and for a while some of the more sophisticated Nazis tried to stress the "Nordic" elements in his art to make him palatable to the rank and file. This was doomed to failure, largely due to Alfred Rosenberg's loathing of Barlach and all the name stood for. Equally unsuccessful were attempts to "sell" Barlachs to Hitler: "Take it away!" was the philistine's angry comment.

It is not surprising that there was no place for Barlach's art in a Third Reich which saw in his work the "passive Slavic soul" combined with "an Asiatic brand of Christian culture"—in other words, awareness of pain, sickness and death, of problems that mortals cannot solve. Helmut Lehmann-Haupt correctly concluded that it was not only Hitler's primitive approach to art in general, but also his demand that the arts conjure up the vision of a healthy, successful society, that prompted the exclusion of

7. Shepherd in a Storm
Schaefer im Sturm
Wood

8. Man Berserk
Der Berserker
Bronze

9. **Lonely Man**
Der Einsame
Bronze

the Expressionists and other independent, critically minded artists: "The dictator wants his artists to promote a feeling of belonging; they must promise security through identification with the community, they must glorify the collective aims of society and propagate complete faith in the methods of the totalitarian leaders." [18]

In the fight over Barlach, the moderates were bound to be the losers. In 1934 a celebration on Barlach's behalf was planned by the State Theater at Schwerin, Mecklenburg, but was canceled on very short notice. The following year *Die echten Sedemunds* was produced in Altona; the play received much applause, but was ordered off the boards after just one performance. In 1936 the publishing firm of the artist's friend, Reinhold Piper, issued a book, *Zeichnungen* (Drawings), with an introduction by the well-known literary man, Paul Fechter. The edition was confiscated by the Gestapo, in an action based on a law for "the Protection of the German Reich." The charge was that the contents of the book were "of such nature as to endanger public security and order." Upon inquiry, the publisher was told that the step had been taken because the "bolshevistic contents of the book were the expression of a destructive conception of art not in keeping with the present era and calculated to endanger the cultural policies of National Socialism." When the publisher pleaded to be allowed at least to sell copies outside Germany, the reply was that this would be "detrimental to the reputation of German art abroad." All copies the Gestapo could lay their hands on were destroyed. In the same year works by Barlach included in the bicentennial jubilee exhibition of the Academy in Berlin were removed by government order.

The climax came in 1937, the year in which both the *Geistkaempfer* and the "Hovering Angel" at Guestrow were taken down. The artist was confidentially "advised" to quit the Academy "voluntarily"; he was expressly forbidden to exhibit (the term used was "*Ausstellungsverbot*") and the threat that he might even be prohibited, like the painter Emil Nolde, from doing any work ("*Berufsausuebungsverbot*") hung over his head.

33

This year 1937 was the "*schlimme Jahr*" (terrible year), as Barlach called it, in the summer of which the "*Entartete Kunst*" (degenerate art) exhibition was held in Munich; everything that was anathema to Hitler was represented in the old arcades of the Hofgarten, there to be jeered at, while on the opposite side of the street in the large, newly built Haus der Deutschen Kunst, insipidly fashioned like a Greek temple, could be admired works by the nonentities who docilely subscribed to the official aesthetic tenets of the Party.

Along with works by other important artists Barlach's *Das Wiedersehen* (The Reunion) was exposed to the little man's laughter. (It was the bronze version confiscated from the Museum at Kiel, one of the three hundred eighty-one Barlachs—a number that included many graphics—seized from German public institutions as part of the campaign to purge them of undesirable art.) The Nazis referred to this profoundly religious work, inspired by the story of Christ's return from the dead and the recognition by Doubting Thomas, as "two monkeys in night shirts." Barlach's book, *Zeichnungen,* was exhibited in a glass case, unopened, lest the public see one of the drawings and form an independent opinion.[19]

This campaign of persecution (of which only a few instances are given here) naturally affected the health of the sexagenarian. His old heart ailment flared up. To make conditions worse the very people of Guestrow who a little earlier had taken pride in the fact that Germany's greatest sculptor was honoring them by dwelling in their midst now yielded to the incessant anti-Barlach propaganda. When he walked the streets, people looked away or even looked through him, pretending not to notice him. Worse yet, hoodlums smashed the windows of his studio. He received "threats written on postal cards," while to his door was fastened "scraps of paper with defamations of me and my dear ones," all anonymous.

Fortunately, his dear ones now included, in addition to son Nikolaus, Marga Boehmer, an understanding and helpful companion in those years of terror. She was the divorced wife of

11. The Vision
Die Vision
Wood

Barlach's assistant, Bernhard A. Boehmer, a double-faced man who catered to the Nazi hierarchy by selling them paintings, while using his influence to protect some of his master's works that were threatened.[20] Barlach could also still talk or write frankly to a few remaining trustworthy friends, among them the journalists and editors Carl Albert Lange, Paul Schurek and Hugo Sieker, all anti-Nazis, from whom he did not have to conceal his loathing of the regime. He told them that in his opinion the Reichstag Fire had been staged; he talked contemptuously about the racism that had labeled him Jewish to destroy him. He complained about the barbaric tone that had become fashionable in the Third Reich: the German radio reminded him of the time when, as a soldier, he had been shouted at by his superiors, and he confessed he was glad to switch to any foreign station, since there civilized attitudes still prevailed. To Reinhold Piper he expressed his revulsion:

"These stirring times don't agree with us. My little boat is sinking fast. . . . I wear no nationalist get-up; noise upsets me. The louder the 'Heils' roar, instead of cheering and raising my arm in Roman attitudes, the more I pull my hat down over my eyes . . ."

He was not idle, not even in that worst of all years, 1937. To the plaster version of a sculpture of a young, extremely gaunt and tragic woman, he gave the very significant title, *Das schlimme Jahr* (The Evil Year). He repeated in wood a work already existing in a bronze version, *Der Zweifler* (The Doubter), giving it his own face. His last wood carving, *Lachende Alte* (Laughing Old Woman), also originated in 1937. Nor was he, contrary to common belief, poverty-stricken in his last years, thanks to a few intrepid patrons, particularly Hamburg's "cigarette king," Hermann F. Reemtsma, who were eager to acquire his works, knowing in their hearts that the day would come when Barlachs would be appreciated again all over Germany.

Still, the artist's letters were filled with the darkest pessimism. Stubbornly he was resolved to stay on "even if they club me to death here." During the *schlimme Jahr* he wrote: "I shall not

12. The Walker
Der Spaziergaenger
Bronze

leave the country. . . . I can see no salvation for me in that, even if I should be successful and have all the things usually characteristic of a good life. . . . A man can be forced to flee, but I shudder when I contemplate that in exile one can also become exiled from one's self or wither away in homelessness." This was a reference to efforts by friends abroad to persuade him to quit Germany. A foreign artist who visited him on their behalf reported that in the middle of the conversation Barlach suddenly got up in fright, looked out of the window and then into the next room to make sure he was not being spied upon. His persecution complex had grown to such dimensions that he decided to bury some of his manuscripts in his garden, even though they actually had no bearing on politics.

Gradually his incentive to work diminished. While he somehow kept busy to the very end, he remarked that it no longer mattered whether he added one or two more pieces to his *oeuvre*, since, after all, he was not allowed to go on working on his "Community of Holy Ones." Finally on August 16, 1938, Barlach, aged sixty-eight, decided that he no longer could endure staying in Germany: "I am selling my property," he wrote to Piper. "I shall go wherever it is possible to work for a few more years at an adequate level."

But he took no action, since his health was very poor. A cure which he had taken in the Hartz mountains had brought little more than temporary relief. In September his heart ailment became so severe that he had to go into a private hospital at Rostock, Mecklenburg. On Monday, October 24, 1938, he was dead.

iv

It was not to be expected that the German state would send representatives to the memorial meeting that took place in the studio on October 27, nor that any of the *gleichgeschaltete* (co-ordinated) artist organizations would despatch delegates. But it was shameful how few of his own colleagues who were not Nazi sympathizers had the *Zivilcourage* to participate. The names of three who did come shall be mentioned here: they were the painter Leopold von Koenig, the sculptor Gerhard Marcks and, of course, Frau Kollwitz. One must have lived under the Nazi dictatorship to appreciate that even this entirely nonpolitical meeting of free spirits was a demonstration against everything the term National Socialism implied. The aged Kollwitz, herself outlawed by the regime, recorded her impressions:

"I entered through a side door and came upon his work table with its assemblage of tools, with some of his works standing against it. As I turned to one side, toward the studio room proper, I saw Barlach lying in the open coffin. The coffin stood in the middle of the room. His bier was solemnly and expensively decorated. He lay with head turned completely to one side, as though to conceal himself. The arms extended and the hands folded together, very small and thin.[21] All around against the walls, his

silent figures. Behind the coffin, a heap of pine boughs. Above the coffin, the mask of the Guestrow cathedral angel. His small dog kept running around the coffin and sniffing at it.

"The ceremony was held over the closed coffin. Pastor Schwartzkopf, who spent eight years in Guestrow and was close to Barlach, delivered the sermon. A good one, and very solemn. He began with Julius Rupps' aphorism: 'Eternity is still.' [22] Then passages from the Book of Job, passages from Barlach's letters and books. The struggle, the search, the cry for God.

"Then a friend spoke a farewell in Low German, then another friend, and finally Gerhard Marcks spoke for the younger artists: 'Let your star be our guiding star.'

"The younger men carried Barlach's coffin to the house adjoining the studio. The day after, he was buried in his home town."

Ratzeburg, where the coffin was lowered into a grave near that of his father,[23] was the town where he had spent the happiest years of his youth, and in his last will he had specified that he wanted to be buried there rather than in Guestrow where he had encountered so much hostility. The grave, in a wooded spot, is now marked by a cast of the *Singing Monk*.

The battle over Barlach continued in the years to come, during which a war more devastating than anything the world had known before was to rage through Barlach's native land, and a dozen other lands as well. His death failed to make his enemies reconsider their stand. *Das schwarze Corps*, organ of the notorious SS (Elite Guard), in a lengthy "necrology"—it appeared under the title, "Was Barlach a Cultural Bolshevist?"—described him as an un-German, Slavic, unbalanced person, whose figures were reminiscent of lunatics. Newspaper obituaries, on the other hand, were not permitted to go beyond ten lines. There were a few brave souls who dared to resist. Theodor Heuss, who was to become president of the German Federal Republic after the war, gave a true picture of Barlach, but could publish it only in a small magazine that somehow managed to function surreptitiously in the Third Reich. Freiburg's Catholic bishop led a prayer for the soul of the Protestant sculptor.

42

14. The Abandoned Ones · *Die Verlassenen* · Wood

15. Migrants
Wandersleute
Wood

In 1939 Hermann F. Reemtsma printed the texts of the speeches delivered at the memorial meeting, along with the messages of condolence sent by Barlach's admirers and friends. (It was a small, anti-Nazi "Who's Who in Germany".) In the same year pieces of Barlach's early prose were printed, also privately, through the efforts of friends under the title, *Fragmente aus sehr frueher Zeit* (Fragments from a Very Early Period). A publisher in Berlin issued an album of Barlach's pencil and pen-and-ink sketches illustrating *Michael Kohlhaas*, Heinrich von Kleist's narrative about a brave and independent seeker of justice. The war was already raging in Europe when the same publisher prepared an edition of the *Russisches Tagebuch* (Russian Diary). Though this was an utterly nonpolitical description of travel undertaken thirty-odd years earlier, this time the Gestapo felt it had to intervene, and the printed pages were destroyed before they could be sent to the bindery. The text of this work has survived, yet some of Barlach's drawings, sculptures and prints were irretrievably lost in the period 1933–1945. Our losses would have been greater, had not friends of the artist found safe hiding places for certain of his most controversial works. While, for instance, the original of the Angel of Guestrow was melted down for ammunition,[24] the Nazis luckily did not get hold of the replica that was made by Barlach himself and concealed by a friend.

Though largely ignored in the books that appeared in the Third Reich, Barlach lived on in the memory of thousands who shared neither Hitler's ideology nor his aesthetics. May 7, 1945 brought relief to them, even though the fall of Nazism was accompanied with hunger, poverty and the disruption of all lines of communication in the devastated cities. To these people, who could breathe freely again after a dozen horrible years, the late Barlach was often a symbol of that undaunted spirit of freedom that no dictator is able to kill.[25] Hamburg, where the resistance to Nazism had been greatest, was the first German city to give Barlach his proper share of *Wiedergutmachung* (restitution). There, late in 1945, while thousands were freezing and starving in the countless ruins, a local theater dared to produce *Dor tote*

16. The Village Fiddler
Der Dorfgeiger
Wood

Tag. In 1946 Paul Schurek, with *Begegnungen mit Ernst Barlach* issued by a publisher in Hamburg, started the long list of books on the master that were to roll from the presses in Western as well as Eastern Germany (the Communist German Democratic Republic). Hamburg is also the seat of the Barlach Society which since 1946 has been issuing for its members annual pamphlets containing selected writings by or about the master.

One after another Barlach memorials to World War I left their hiding places and came back to the towns where they had been

17. The Avenger
Der Raecher
Bronze

18. The Ecstatic One
Der Ekstatiker
Wood

before.[26] All over Germany museums now proudly displayed whatever works by Barlach they had kept in the vaults during the bad years or had been able to acquire—or reacquire—since May 1945. Luckily neither the home nor the studio at Guestrow suffered much from the Russian occupation of the city. In the studio Friedrich Schult, who had acted as a kind of Boswell to the master, arranged a permanent exhibition of Barlach's works, while Marga Boehmer installed other works in the Gertrude's Chapel, an old church no longer used for worship. These Barlachs were perfectly safe in Guestrow even though at one point Stalinist critics in the German Democratic Republic assailed Barlach's work as being "strongly dominated by anti-democratic tendencies" and as "an example of the crisis of ugliness in art." Apparently Barlach is not the proper spiritual fare for a dictatorship, whether of the left or right. Two important writers, Bertolt Brecht and Arnold Zweig, however, dared to pay homage to him in the face of the prevailing party line. Currently in the more or less "de-Stalinized" East Germany Barlach is almost unanimously appreciated as a socialist, patriot and humanist.

In the German Federal Republic (West Germany) there are now two places entirely dedicated to the memory of the master. One is the small *Gedenkstaette* (memorial), a one-room museum at Ratzeburg under the direction of Nikolaus Barlach, located in the old house the Barlachs occupied from 1877 to 1884. The other is the spacious and utterly modern Barlach-Haus, built in 1961 on the outskirts of Hamburg; there the vast collection acquired over the years by the late Reemtsma is sheltered and made admirably accessible to the public. How widely respected and loved Barlach is now in his native country was proven by the reverberating echoes of the commemoration in 1963 of the twenty-fifth anniversary of his death. While German art has inevitably gone far beyond the pre-World War I tenets held by this master, newspapers, radio and television programs, and, of course, museums and galleries demonstrate that his work is still considered a valuable aid to mankind in its unceasing struggle for spiritual renewal.

19. Freezing Girl
Frierendes Maedchen
Wood

20. The Man Pilloried
Der Mann im Stock
Wood

Strange that man does not want to know that his father is God.

From THE DEAD DAY

V

Nearly all of Germany's Expressionists had literary talent: they wrote poems, plays, novels, manifestoes and autobiography. Yet none of these had so clear a *Doppelbegabung* (double gift) as Barlach, none commanded equal vigor and persuasiveness in the written word and in the various plastic media. Thus, while the literary contributions of his colleagues may be treated in a paragraph or two as the side lines of professional artists, a chapter is not enough to deal adequately with the thousands of pages Barlach filled with striking words sprung from his deepest feelings.

However, we will dwell here only briefly on Barlach the poet, dramatist, writer of letters, essays and narrative prose. For one thing the chief task of this volume is to introduce Barlach's sculptures, drawings and prints to the American public. Moreover, only a fraction of his literary work is available in English, and even those somewhat familiar with the German language will find it hard to plough through certain of his works—especially some of the plays—written as they are in an idiosyncratic style with a nonconformist syntax and grammar and with a vocabulary that not only often borrows heavily from Low German dialect, but even includes terms apparently coined by the master himself.

A fleeting glance at his literary *oeuvre* is nonetheless essential.

21. The Law Giver (also called Moses)
Der Gesetzgeber, auch Moses benannt
Wood

It occupies three substantial volumes, the first of which contains his plays, while his prose and a few excursions into poetry are divided between the remaining two. To the biographer his extant letters—well over a thousand—are of paramount importance. Three different selections from these letters have been published so far. The complete edition of his letters, superseding the previous compilations, is still in preparation at the time of this writing.

The letters are informal, definitely written without an eye for publication. Only in a few cases, where circumstances demanded it, is the diction formal, or the tone didactic. They contain amazingly little about art, but a good many references to literature. Barlach rarely mentions his sculpture; he is more apt to refer to his plays. The various places he visited in Germany or abroad are vividly described. Above all, he speaks often about his loved ones, especially his son. He is overwhelmed by his loneliness as he stands apart from the busy market life of the big, overactive cities, and hints at his incessant struggle to discover and express his own true self. But he is never defeatist, and, no matter what happens to him, he is innocent of self-pity. In these communications, ranging from greetings on postcards to lengthy epistles, his charming, unaggressive humor also comes through, as does his faith in the inherent goodness of man.

More clues to the development of his art can be found in the autobiographical sketch, *Ein selbsterzaehltes Leben* (A Self-told Life), which is also full of subtle humor surprising in a tortured man with an apostolic air about him. Most of what we know concerning the master's youth, his early joys and worries, his family and friends, stems from these forty-odd delightful pages. The sketch reveals a great deal about the passionate young man and frustrated, slightly confused artist up to his return from his second stay in Paris, but, though it was written in 1927, it stops with the artist's pivotal agreement with Paul Cassirer in 1910.

Like *Selbsterzaehltes Leben*, Barlach's *Eine Steppenfahrt* (A Journey through the Steppe), a fruit of his experiences in Southern Russia and based to a degree on his Russian diary, *Russisches*

23. Hooded Beggar Woman
Verhuellte Bettlerin
Wood

24. The Blind Man Carrying the Halt
Der Blinde traegt den Lahmen
Clay

25. Ecstatic Woman
Ekstatische Frau
Bronze

Tagebuch, was also published during his lifetime; illustrated with Barlach's own lithographs, it appeared in a German art magazine. There are also a few short essays which Barlach himself wrote for publication and which were printed in newspapers or books during the Weimar Republic, among them a humorous fictitious dialogue between the painter Max Liebermann and a somewhat naïve admiring bystander. More than nine-tenths of his prose, however, became known only after 1945. This includes numerous short fragments jotted down at a time when Barlach still considered himself primarily a writer; [27] they are charming, unassuming and unpretentious compositions, often deriving inspiration from the streets of Paris or the plains of Holstein, the amusing, largely autobiographical soliloquies of a romantic dreamer. The diary Barlach painstakingly kept at Guestrow during World War I demonstrates the civilian's maturing attitudes towards the event—from enthusiasm to skepticism and finally to disgust with the holocaust—and also provides insight into his relationships with his mother and his son, and a picture of life in a small North German town.

Of the utmost importance are several long essays written between 1929 and 1937, but never published until after the war, in which the artist replies to the attacks made upon him first by the *Stahlhelm* and then by the Nazis: far from apologetic when accused of being "alienated" from the cultural traditions of his land, he points out how deeply rooted he was in everything German, without ever denying his indebtedness to the spirit and civilization of the non-German world. In this category of outstanding "political" documents also belongs Barlach's radio address of 1933; the text, based on a typescript found among his papers after his death, was like many other writings made public by the Barlach Society of Hamburg.

The large fragments of novels, *Seespeck* (this is the hero's name) and particularly *Der gestohlene Mond* (The Stolen Moon), tax the patience of any reader unaccustomed to narratives without neatly developed and finally solved plots. Both are very loosely constructed, or, perhaps, not constructed at all. The former, an excerpt of which appeared in 1920,[28] deals with an intellectual who in certain ways resembles the author, and who sharply observes the picturesque characters Barlach encountered in the Lower Elbe region. The locale of *Der gestohlene Mond* is a small town, modeled, perhaps, after Guestrow and inhabited by peculiar people, among them the two dissimilar twins, Wau and Wahl. Both works are filled with scenes of a rather baroque humor. Admirers have compared the second work, an unusual and difficult piece of prose, with fiction by Franz Kafka, Robert Musil, Alfred Doeblin and Hermann Broch, representatives of the new surrealist and irrational trend that buried the traditional novel; others have frankly admitted their inability to grasp its meaning.

Critics are also divided about the merits of Barlach's plays. He completed seven; they were published—three of them with illustrations by the author—under the imprint of Paul Cassirer between 1922 and 1929; an unfinished drama, *Der Graf von Ratzeburg* (The Count of Ratzeburg), was not printed until 1951. Thomas Mann, for one, extolled the "genuine folk poetry" in these plays. After seeing on the stage *Die echten Sedemunds*, Kaethe Kollwitz confided to her diary, "a deep sense of envy that Barlach is so much more profound than I." A celebrated critic of the Weimar Republic, Arthur Eloesser, wrote that Barlach's characters resembled figures carved in wood: "They are like anonymous sufferers in some tragedy of humanity, and go muffled in their sorrows as though in a heavy mantle laid upon their shoulders by fate."

Several of these plays were performed on the German stage before the last war. But they had only short runs, and never more than *Achtungserfolg* (critical success). While they have plots of a sort, they are not developed with the strict logic to be found in the theater of Schiller or Ibsen which is generally preferred by audiences. They are loosely woven, more poetic than dramatic. Above all, like the dramas of other Expressionists such as Toller, Hasenclever, Von Unruh or Barlach's fellow artist, the still living

26. Old Woman Dancing
Tanzende Alte
Bronze

27. The Fugitive
Der Fluechtling
Bronze

painter Oskar Kokoschka, they employ a disconcerting explosive language, that, most of the time, irritates the listener. Hence they lent themselves to a misunderstanding and misinterpretation that were a constant source of vexation to their author. Though a sort of grotesque humor is not absent, they are for the most part like nightmarish dreams. They are filled with ideas so complex as to require of the audience too much thinking and rethinking on the spot, and the result is often discomfort and even bewilderment.

Even in the plays set in ordinary little German towns at the turn of the century the characters are—contrary to the author's assertion—not real people, though the dialect they use is real enough. Man's spiritual growth, Man's metaphysical anguish, Man's relationship to God, and the inevitable triumph of the spirit over materialism are the universal and timeless issues with which Barlach is concerned.

In *Der tote Tag* (The Dead Day) a mother vainly tries to keep her son from maturing to manhood and from finding his estranged father who, as becomes manifest at the end, is the Spirit, is God. *Der arme Vetter* (The Poor Cousin) is a tormented dreamer who by committing suicide drives another person to a more spiritual life. *Die echten Sedemunds* (The Genuine Sedemunds) reveals the philistine inhabitants of a small town in all their apathy to higher values. *Der Findling* (The Foundling) deals with a miracle that, through the healing powers of love, turns an ugly little creature into a radiantly beautiful child. In *Die Suendflut* (The Flood) God himself, in the guise of a beggar, wanders through a vice-ridden world. The main character of *Der blaue Boll* (The Blue Boll) is a wealthy, pleasure-seeking country squire named Boll, who through shattering experiences gains a new insight into the meaning of life. Barlach's last completed play, *Die gute Zeit* (The Good Time), takes us to a utopian society on an island in the Mediterranean where the characters discover that the good time they expected is unachievable. In the unfinished *Graf von Ratzeburg* the hero, a religious man, makes a pilgrimage to the Holy Land to find his true path and true goal.

Barlach probably did not intend to write *Lesedramen* (plays to be read). He wrote for the stage and felt that his plays were suited to it, or, at least, to a stage of the future where the productions would not run counter to their spirit. In the nineteen-twenties the lithographs or woodcuts he created for three of the plays were more admired than these and all of the other plays; the audiences and the theater Barlach might have anticipated arrived only after the last war. To judge by the new critics, Barlach the playwright has at least reached his goal, so far as the avant-garde is concerned. Outside Germany many who never heard of the sculptor Barlach suddenly learned of the existence of a very prominent dramatist Barlach. In 1959 H. F. Garten wrote: "Barlach stands as one of the pre-eminent exponents of what may be called the mystic or religious type of expressionist drama. . . . His concerns were the timeless issues of human existence, the triumph of the spirit over the encroaching materialism of our age." [29]

Martin Esslin in 1961 declared that Barlach's "haunting plays . . . anticipate some of the dreamlike, mythical features of the Theatre of the Absurd." [30] Indeed, like Ionesco, Beckett, Albee and others, Barlach unpredictably fuses tragedy with humor, the real with the unreal, employing a language totally different from that heard in the commercial theater.

Unfortunately, recent performances, such as that of *Die echten Sedemunds* at the Deutsches Schauspielhaus in Hamburg, did not bear out the prediction of enthusiasts who had assumed that the day of Barlach the dramatist had arrived. Was it the fault of the staging again that little more than an *Achtungserfolg* was achieved?

Whatever the evaluation of Barlach as a contributor to the theater, the plays, fascinating in themselves, are complementary to his art. One is reminded of the interrelationship between the medieval mystery plays and the carvings of saints made for the churches and cathedrals. Unquestionably the anonymous playwrights influenced the anonymous craftsmen, and vice versa, just as there exists a subtle affinity between the figures Barlach carved in words with those he carved in wood.

28. The Procuress II
Die Kupplerin II
Bronze

29. Old Woman with a Flask
Die Alte mit der Flasche
Clay

VI

Have I ever illustrated a text? I have merely offered interpretations.

Odilon Redon

Significantly, the post-Barlach generation treasures most in Barlach's vast production what, by and large, constitutes only preliminary studies for the work that made him famous during his lifetime. With today's emphasis on the spontaneous and informal, Barlach's drawings are often preferred to his more carefully executed creations, and among these drawings the favored ones are mere sketches that appear to have emerged rapidly from some dark cranny below the threshold of consciousness. Whether or not this current love for the "unfinished" is a dangerous fad, one is glad to share the current delight in Barlach's draftsmanship. He was one of the outstanding draftsmen of his generation, and drawing occupied nearly as much of his time as sculpture. Prints, too, are in a sense drawings, and he acted as a draftsman even with a burin, when he carved a design into wood, or when he made a lithographic crayon rush over a transfer paper.

Barlach would not have been so German an artist had not the graphic arts occupied an important place in his *oeuvre*. The art historian, Max Dvořák, made much of the fact that plastic expression in black and white was held in higher regard in northern countries than in the South of Europe:

"It would be just as futile to write a history of Greek thought that ignored Greek tragedy as it would be impossible to present a history of German art without devoting one of its most important chapters to graphic art." In Albrecht Duerer, Germany had one of the world's greatest draftsmen and printmakers of all time, and there were outstanding German graphic artists shortly before and shortly after Duerer. In the 19th century Germany, though it had an Adolf von Menzel, was not on a par with the France of Jean-Auguste-Dominique Ingres. Draftsmanship, however, recovered from its lull with the arrival of Kollwitz, Barlach, Alfred Kubin and the artists generally called *Expressionisten*. A century earlier Goethe had pointed out the importance of drawings: far from being just steps on the way to the finished masterpieces (prints, sculptures or paintings) they were, he said, "invaluable" because they gave the purest "mental intention" of the artist, and also because they conveyed "the mood of his mind at the very moment of creation."

Nonetheless artists were, and perhaps in some cases still are, divided as to the desirability of displaying their drawings publicly. It is true that Duerer signed and even dated many of his drawings, sold them to patrons or gave them to friends. Many of the old masters, however, regarded their drawings as mere preparation for the "real thing" and rarely signed what they considered ephemeral sketches, retaining them (if they did so at all) classified by subject as craftsmen kept sample books. Gauguin refused to let critics see his drawings: "They are my private letters, my secrets." Even among the moderns there are some who have not been willing to exhibit their drawings.

Barlach, however, held a different view. While he did not always sign his drawings and rarely dated them, he did not hide them, and even submitted a selection to the public in the volume *Zeichnungen*, whose fate has been described in an earlier chapter. Altogether, more than a thousand of his drawings, the majority done in charcoal, the others in pencil, chalks, pen-and-

30. Standing Peasant Woman
Stehende Baeuerin
Wood

32. The Young Woman
Das junge Weib
Wood

ink or in mixed media, sometimes touched with washes, have come down to us. This represents only a fraction of the drawings he did in his long life, since, like all other artists, he discarded or lost much of what he produced. Throughout his career he considered drawing a *Ding an sich* rather than a mere preparation for more ambitious work; for him, drawing was a psychic catharsis, and in his drawings he often revealed his strongest feelings and his deepest thought.

The schools Barlach attended stressed drawing far more than do academies today. The spirit of Monsieur Ingres—who held that drawing was "the probity of art" and that it took thirty years to learn to draw—still prevailed in Europe's educational system towards the end of the last century, whether the doddering teachers there were direct pupils of Ingres or not. The *Gewerbeschule* in Hamburg was no exception. Lyonel Feininger, who had come from New York, and who studied at the school early in 1888, leaving about the time Barlach enrolled, wrote that he would draw from plaster casts of old sculpture for eight hours each day, until, in order to spare his eyes, he had to reduce his hours to six. Even the painting class was basically an academy of drawing. In the same school Barlach learned to master on paper fifty different kinds of garment folds. Since drawing from the nude was not offered at the school, students would privately hire a model to practice what is called *Aktzeichnen* in German.

But this training failed to damage him. In Paris the twenty-year-old Barlach felt "at home in the shadow of the draftsman Steinlen," a reference to Théophile-Alexandre Steinlen, vigorous cartoonist for numerous newspapers, imaginative illustrator of books, and maker of posters, who sympathetically and realistically interpreted the plight of the proletariat in the French capital. Whatever proficiency as a draftsman Barlach may have acquired at the academies of Germany and France, there is nothing "academic" about his drawings. Even in the earliest extant samples they have a swiftness and freedom linking them to the best in late 19th-century French art, especially Steinlen's, rather than to the hard and precise draftsmanship that prevailed in Bismarck's Germany.

The stylization of the decorative *Art Nouveau* which subordinated natural forms to a two-dimensional rhythmicality is often noticeable in his early work. More frequent, however, is an uninhibited realism that tries to capture fugitive moments and situations—in beer gardens, streets, on trains, in cafés or theaters. If at first he expressed himself in a maze of loose and scratchy scribbles, one day he discovered that he could achieve in three lines what had previously required ten.

The draftsman Barlach "found" himself earlier than the sculptor. Even the commercial work done around 1900 for satirical weeklies is superior to his sculpture commissioned by his bourgeois patrons, which conforms precisely to the prevailing middle-class notion of what sculpture should be. In the cartoons for *Jugend* and *Simplizissimus* [31] he was drawing for anti-militarist, anti-bourgeois, anti-Hohenzollern periodicals, and could, at least, share the editors' democratic and humanist leanings. Sympathizing with the Social Democratic opposition to the Emperor and the ruling classes, he drew with vigor in his cartoons the wretchedness of metropolitan slums, often disclosing a reality as terrible as some of the scenes described by Dickens in *Oliver Twist*. A typical pen-and-ink drawing contributed to *Simplizissimus* shows three arrogant frock-coated gentlemen walking over wretched underground dwellings from which emaciated faces and hands emerge. The biting caption of this cartoon, entitled *The Farsighted Members of the Commission Report,* reads: ". . . as far as the eye reaches it meets with scenes of happiness and contentment."

In the Ukraine he filled his sketchbooks with pictures in which the tragic, monumental, Dostoevskian traits are stronger than the whimsical and the grotesque. For the next thirty-two years he continued this sketching *naer het leven* (from life), to use the three words Pieter Brueghel the Elder inscribed on his studies of rustic figures. Yet the majority of Barlach's drawings, particularly the later ones, are not as dependent on everyday reality as is

33. **Cloaked Man**
Mann mit dem Mantel
Wood

Brueghel's graphic work. They are mostly points of departure for future flights into the land between the conscious and the unconscious, between the visible and the invisible, between waking and dreaming, that was Barlach's regular habitat.

Indeed, the more valuable among his drawings were made at night without any subject before him, after he was through with his sculptural work, at a time when most men allow themselves the luxuries of peaceful family life, or the diversions of theater, movie or social gathering. Rodin would not draw without the stimulus of a nude model sitting or walking around in his studio. Barlach's drawings, however, are mainly the dreams of a somnambulist whose hand races over a piece of paper, or the monologues of one struggling with the invisible angel. Through these drawings—unpremeditated, spontaneous—he was able to release inner images, freeing his subconscious mind from havoc-wreaking tormentors.

If the practitioners of art can be divided into realists and surrealists, the mature Barlach clearly belongs with the surrealists. If asked to choose between Courbet who said challengingly, "I'll paint an angel when you can show me one," and Blake who sang, "I hear a voice you cannot hear . . . I see a hand you cannot see," Barlach would have chosen Blake. Redon's statement that his own originality consisted in "making incredible beings live according to credible laws, in placing the logic of the possible at the service of the invisible" might very well be applied to the graphic work of Barlach. Barlach's goals were also well expressed by a German of his own generation, Franz Marc: "We are today seeking behind the veil of nature's outward appearance hidden things which seem to us more important than the discoveries of the impressionists. . . . Art . . . is the bridge into the spirit world."

Witches, furies and a variety of macabre phenomena such as Dances of Death abound in his graphic work. Demons may press an artist, but he does not succumb to them. Instead, he may vanquish them by his craft, just as the prehistoric hunter killed his fear of powerful wild animals by drawing their likenesses on cave

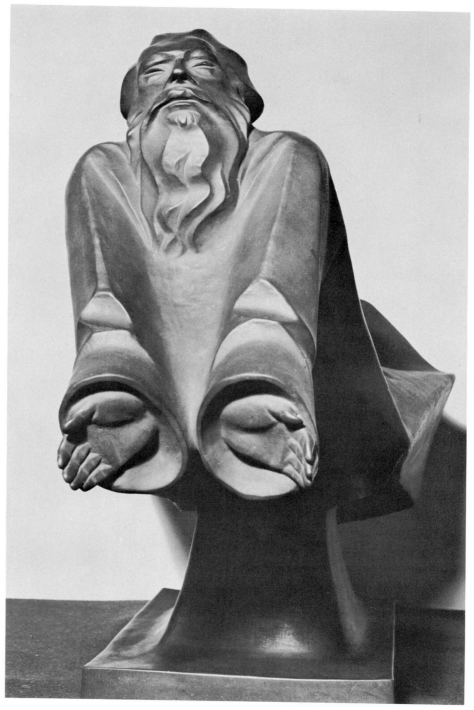

34. God the Father Hovering
Schwebender Gottvater
Terra cotta

35. Sleeping Pair *Zwei Schlafende*
Wood

36. **Detail of**
Plate 35

walls. If he cannot conquer his demon, he often takes the sting out of it by letting us look straight into its horrifying face.

Some of his drawings may be characterized as "grotesque"; they might be compared to the fantastic outpourings of some of his contemporaries, such as Feininger, Kubin or Klee. But he did not always dwell in the "grottoes" of darkness from which this term is derived. With a tenderness and humility not surprising in one whose Christianity was close in spirit to that of the early followers of Christ, he drew scenes inspired by episodes from the Old and the New Testament, and the dramatis personae of the Bible. While the sculptor rarely permitted friends to sit for portrait busts and never made one of himself, in his graphic work portraits and self-portraits abound. There is, of course, nothing "photographic" about them. Barlach always insisted that the outward appearance of a man was only a mask, and that he had to look behind it; he wanted to show what he felt and sensed rather than what he actually saw.

Many of these drawings are "sculptural" rather than linear: strokes inside and outside the contour, crosshatchings, shadings give the illusion of three-dimensionality. This is particularly true of those that are *Vorzeichnungen*, studies anticipating sculptures to come. In many cases, however, there is only a loose connection between a particular drawing and the sculpture for which it appears to prepare. The numerous sketches for the *Geistkaempfer* demonstrate that only after a long search did the artist arrive at the final solution to be executed in clay, and ultimately cast in bronze.[32] On the other hand, many of his drawings have a historical and documentary value because they acquaint us with the general outline of a sculpture known to have existed but now irretrievably lost. Certain sculptures, which never saw the light of day due to right-wing and Nazi opposition, exist at least in the *Urbild* (preparatory drawing), especially the war memorial which was for the Pomeranian town of Malchin, or the additional sculptures for the façade of St. Catherine's Church in Luebeck.

Nothing "political" was contained in *Zeichnungen,* the confiscation and eventual destruction of which has been mentioned.

37. Horror
Das Grauen
Wood

38. Pregnant Girl
Schwangeres Maedchen
Wood

But there was something equally "bad" about them—the absence of the blind optimism and deluded self-confidence that the Nazi state had to propagate. For Barlach presented unhappy people: men and women starving, freezing, ailing, mourning; lonely individuals filled with melancholy, with doubt. In Nazi-approved drawings, people smile or show off enormous muscles in heroic determination to fight for victory; Barlach remained "unheroic" to the very end.[33]

Barlach the printmaker stems directly from the draftsman. As a matter of fact, his lithographs, drawn on transfer paper rather than on the stone or zinc plate directly, and done with a special greasy crayon, differ so little from his charcoal drawings that sometimes it is difficult to distinguish one from the other. In his eagerness to reproduce certain of his drawings he did not bother to obtain all the nuances, all the *finesse*, that lithography affords, but contented himself with turning them over to a craftsman who converted them into prints by means of zinc plates.

His woodcuts are a totally different affair. Wood was his favorite medium, he knew all its properties well and he executed his own woodcuts from beginning to end. (By contrast, Duerer and, in the 19th century, Adolf von Menzel, confined themselves to the production of designs which were translated into woodcuts by professional cutters.) While Barlach's lithographs sometimes reflect the inadequacy or impatience of the printer (who, at best, could only approximate the artist's intention), his woodcuts offer us all of himself as much as do his wood sculptures. He made his first woodcut, an illustration for Kleist's *Michael Kohlhaas*, in 1910. He was not the first modern to resuscitate this medium that had long been held in low esteem as "xylography." Gauguin had produced woodcuts in the interval between his two sojourns in the South Seas and again during his second, final stay at Tahiti. Munch, too, had discovered the woodcut years before Barlach, but his woodcuts, filled with color like those of Gauguin, are mainly reworkings of his paintings.

Most of the German Expressionists exploited the woodcut. In fact, one art historian starts his analysis of German Expressionist art with the phrase, "In the beginning there was the woodcut." [34] As for Barlach, he approached the woodcut about three years after he had made his first sculpture in wood. He wrote: "The woodcut demands complete avowal, an unequivocal precipitation of what one really means. It dictates a certain universal expression and rejects an amiable or easy solution." He patiently wrestled with the refractory material, a task that required strict discipline. (It was not suitable when he needed quick release for his nervous energy; on such occasions he resorted to charcoal, pencil or ink.) While the medium imposes limitations upon the artist, at the same time it permits the heightening of emotional tensions through the contrasts between heavy blacks and stark whites that produce a creative dialogue. Few other artists make us realize as fully as Barlach that white can be a stark, cruel color or a tender and lyrical one, and that black can be soft or dramatic, deep or brittle. The woodcut was the appropriate medium for an introspective man who constantly asked questions concerning life and death, and who always sought the essential in human beings, but also for one who had a certain kinship to the medieval humorist and prankster, Till Eulenspiegel. (Incidentally, Till died, according to tradition, at Moelln, a town very near Ratzeburg, where Barlach is buried.)

When Kaethe Kollwitz first saw Barlach's woodcuts in 1920, they "knocked her over" and inspired her to turn to this technique. Like Barlach (but unlike Kirchner, Heckel and others) she dispensed with color.

The wise Erasmus might have written about Barlach what he wrote about Duerer:

> What does he not express in monochromes, that is, in lines of black? Light, dark, splendor, eminence, depressions and, although they derive from one single printing, several aspects are presented to the eye of the spectator. These he arranges in the most significant lines, yet if you should add color you would injure the work. And is it not more wonderful to accomplish without the blandishment of color?

In his *catalogue raisonné* entitled *Das graphische Werk*, the indefatigable Friedrich Schult lists and illustrates nearly three hundred works by Barlach. Cassirer had the courage to issue several collections of his prints, nearly all of them with texts by either Barlach or other poets. The prints are either interspersed in the text or gathered in separate portfolios, and in most cases there are both expensive de luxe editions for bibliophiles, and more modestly priced popular editions. Lithographs embellish Barlach's first drama, *Der tote Tag*, as well as the second, *Der arme Vetter*. Lithographs are to be found in a book containing

39. Group of three Figures; also called Death · *Gruppe aus drei Figuren; auch Der Tod* · Bronze

selected poems by Goethe. Barlach contributed woodcuts to a long poem, *Der Kopf* (The Head) by a now forgotten Expressionist, Reinhold von Walter (who in 1929 issued the first evaluation of Barlach to appear in book form). There are woodcuts for Barlach's fourth drama, *Der Findling,* and for an edition of the witch-haunted *Walpurgisnacht* (a scene from the first part of Goethe's *Faust*) and for one of Schiller's triumphant odes *An die Freude* (To Joy). Eight woodcuts, without text, were gathered together under a title selected by the publisher, *Die Wandlungen Gottes* (Transformations of God). Since copies of all editions are now extremely rare, available, at best, only at special auctions, publishers in West Germany have begun to reissue the old books and albums for a new audience.

There are many woodcuts, and even more lithographs, that are outside these cycles. The last woodcut (1928) was the awe-inspiring *Moses auf Sinai* (Moses on Mount Sinai). The artist who had first turned to lithography about 1903, created his last work in this medium in 1932. This was *Der neue Tag* (The New Day), a picture of two angels blowing horns "with the energy of a Harlem swing band," as a reviewer put it. These two prints and many others by Barlach can be found in many a print room in museums all over the United States. Thus, while it is necessary to travel to Barlach's native country to see much of his sculpture, his graphic work can be viewed here without much difficulty. Barlach's graphic work is beyond and above any national boundaries, and not in a physical sense only. However deeply rooted it may be in the soil of the German lands, in its ramifications it reaches, like a mighty tree, to the sky, to the sun which warms and nourishes all.

. . . My artistic language is the human figure. . . . The things that arrest my attention are what a human being has suffered and is able to endure, his greatness, his concerns. . . .

Barlach (in a letter to a friend)

VII

While Barlach's plays and the two unfinished novels, the bulk of his work as a writer, belong, broadly speaking, to Expressionist literature, and therefore to the twentieth century, the sculptor Barlach has antecedents that go far back in time.[35] There can be no doubt that the sculptor took a long time to find himself. He had none of the precociousness of Michelangelo, whose unusual promise was recognized by the artists and cognoscenti of Florence when he was still a boy of fourteen. Barlach was also not fortunate enough to grow up in a cultural atmosphere as rich in great practitioners of his craft as the late Quattrocento.

When Barlach decided to become an artist, sculpture was at a very low ebb in his native country, which had produced no masters comparable to Rude, Barye or Carpeaux. By 1888, Rodin had completed *The Bronze Age, John the Baptist* and *The Gates of Hell.* Germany, however, could boast only of Reinhold Begas,[36] who with his disciples created huge monuments of emperors and statesmen that combine theatrical poses with a slavish imitation of nature and the most insipidly faithful treatment of banal details. Young Barlach was surrounded by *Kitsch*—and, in his early days, was taught to make *Kitsch.* Little need be said about

40. The Reunion; also called Christ and Thomas
Das Wiedersehen; auch Christus und Thomas
Bronze

41. Detail
of Plate 40

42. Head of the Memorial
Kopf des Ehrenmals
Bronze

43. Guestrow
Memorial
Ehrenmal
Bronze

the few pieces that survive from the period 1888 to 1906. With
the recent re-evaluation of *Art Nouveau*, one is less inclined to
reject at first glance the small decorative items Barlach did for
a ceramic factory, but it is hard to believe that they came from the
hands of the same man who only a few years later would fashion
sculptures as stable, solid and monumentally "abstract" as the
Melon Eater or the *Russian Beggar Woman*.

89

Even Barlach's early drawings evidence an originality that presages the sculptural work he started to create at the age of thirty-six or thirty-seven. So do some of his early writings. Ironically, he knew that neoclassical, academic notions of beauty and charm were not for him. In a letter to his friend Duesel he praised ugliness, demoniacal passion, grotesque geniality and, above all, humor. Thus it seems that the Russian adventure was required to give birth to what the world has ever since recognized admiringly as "Barlach." In his first attempts to get rid of the ballast of the past, bronze and ceramics somehow hampered the master's wish to move away as far as possible from the superficial delightfulness of the prevalent genre sculpture. For what he needed to be "Barlach" was not gloss and smoothness, but unpolished roughness. True, with the ceramic figure of a *Beggar Woman* (1907) the real Barlach does emerge. With her bent back, hooded face and hands extended in a beseeching gesture, she unforgettably expresses the humiliation of asking for charity. A tragic beauty hovers over this work that is so deeply personal, so free from sentimentality and so broadly symbolic. Still the mat surface of the material did not permit him to bring out, as vividly as wood might have allowed him to do, the rugged primitiveness of this unfortunate being from a village street in Russia.

It would be incorrect to assume that once he had found the medium most suited to his needs Barlach never used another. Clay continued to be an important means for creating quick sketches for the making of the final works either in wood or, in some instances, bronze or stone. Sculptural concepts have come down to us in plaster, in bronze and in wood. In two large monuments he very successfully employed bronze: the hovering angel of Guestrow and the *Geistkaempfer* made for Kiel. The three figures for the St. Catherine Church in Luebeck—*Woman in the Wind, Beggar on Crutches,* and *Singing Monk* [37]—were done in *Klinker* (vitrified clay). Still it is accurate to say that Barlach was first and above all a wood carver, and that he overshadowed all of his colleagues who applied themselves to the same medium.

90

As Gauguin was the first modern master to turn to the wood-cut, he can also be credited with having been the first to have redeemed wood as a sculptural medium. At a time when no sculptor in France would use anything but marble or bronze, Gauguin ventured to send to the Sixth Impressionist Exhibition (1881) two wood carvings (a medallion, *La Chanteuse,* and a tiny figure, *La Petite Parisienne*). While in Britanny, he carved clogs, walking sticks, even furniture; on Tahiti he decorated his hut like a pagan temple with his own carvings. But this sculpture was more in the nature of a pastime, as his creative energy was devoted to his paintings and, to a lesser degree, his graphic work. Other French masters followed him in exploring the potentialities of wood. His disciple, Emile Bernard, carved furniture and painted it in gay colors. Among Maillol's earliest sculptures are reliefs carved in wood. Georges Lacombe, the *"Nabi sculpteur,"* carved four decorative reliefs for a bed.

But all of these are minor works. Even to the *Expressionisten* wood offered a minor stimulus only. In a self-portrait of 1905—the year when *Die Bruecke* was founded—young Erich Heckel is seen holding one of his own small wood sculptures. There exist wood sculptures by his associates, Ernst Ludwig Kirchner and Karl Schmidt-Rottluff, indebted like all men of the *Bruecke* to the primitive art they had just discovered at the Ethnological Museum of Dresden. Emil Nolde, having been trained in wood carving, worked in furniture factories as a journeyman; his desire to make use of wood as an artistic medium, however, came rather late—on his journey to the South Seas when he chanced upon the exotic woods used to fuel the steamship boilers and became fascinated by their possibilities. The *Bruecke* painters embellished their simple and inadequate ateliers in Dresden and Berlin with imaginatively carved and painted furniture and thus created a make-believe world of beauty although they were then deep in poverty and want. Two members of the *Blauer Reiter*, Vasily Kandinsky and August Macke, also carved in wood.[38]

Yet all of these were peripheral activities. In Central Europe professional wood carving had declined rapidly after the death

44. **Champion of the Spirit**
Der Geistkaempfer
Bronze

in 1775 of Franz Ignatz Guenther, the last great sculptor of the South German rococo period. It did not disappear completely, but continued on a humble basis, unappreciated by the connoisseurs, as a folk art in remote villages of Austria, Bavaria and Switzerland. Wood carving was, of course, not taught at the schools Barlach attended. Hence, to acquaint himself with the qualities and peculiarities of wood and to learn the use of the necessary tools, he had to turn to a master craftsman who made furniture and household utensils.

As his drawings indicate, Barlach was quick-witted, excitable, impatient, often delighted to hurry a pencil or piece of charcoal with sheer gusto over the surface of a sheet of paper. But he could also muster a great deal of patience when it was required to turn his hasty clay sketches into the less wieldy medium of wood (a medium that would not have suited Rodin, who wanted the children of his imagination to grow quickly). Wood, being a natural and organic growth, struck a responsive chord in the natural man Barlach. He favored oak, though he also used walnut, linden, beech, lime and teak wood. He preferred large blocks, streaked and washed by the rain, to the slick, "perfect" pieces used by commercial artists. Wood was the perfect matrix for his unsuave, unurbane, rustic personality; he learned to know its character and limitations, respected its texture and grain and exploited all its qualities, never camouflaged or overpolished its surface, never disguised its color. Completely oblivious to the necessity for food and rest, as though driven by a demonic force, he would doggedly hammer away at the block for hours, betraying a robust strength unexpected in so small and slender a man. He would choose a block whose shape fitted his idea, a pillar or a cube, visualizing the dormant statue in the primitive shape. Unlike other sculptors, he did not require a professional model: he did not want his shapes to be too "real," to allow details to separate his creation from his emotion.[39]

He attacked the material with thousands of mallet blows, chipping off tiny bits of wood passionately but carefully, until the desired image emerged with the required clarity and sharpness. Barlach did not go out of his way to conceal the marks of his tools; the facets, the countless little planes tracing the work's organic growth under his knowing hands, remain. Through his method of "chip carving" he endowed forms with a vibrant quality missing from the work of more timid men who sought to "vivify" their creations by careful imitation of skin texture, hair and garment.

Barlach has sometimes been called a follower of Gothic sculpture. He certainly knew the 15th-century wood carvings that originally graced small churches in remote towns of Mecklenburg and finally found their way into the Landesmuseum at Schwerin. Together with his publisher, Reinhold Piper, he once visited the cathedral at Guestrow to point out to his friend how impressed he was by the heads of the Apostles, attributed to the master from Luebeck, Claus Berg, and created about 1525. To his friend Schurek he related how impressed he had always been with the Bordesholm Altar in the cathedral of Schleswig made between 1514 and 1521 by Hans Brueggemann, who was also a North German carver: "I could bet that, in order to make his warriors, spectators, all his men and women, he walked through the streets and over the countryside, with the kind of small sketch book that I have."

In an essay, "In praise of being rooted in the soil," [40] written about 1933 as if in reply to attacks by the Nazis, he stated:

> I confess I am the pupil of unknown masters, such as the one of the Christ Crucified, South German, 13th century, at the Germanic Museum, Nuremberg, or the master of another Christ, a Suabian work of the 12th century, ibidem, or the Hungarian Cross of St. Severin at Andernach, by a Cologne Master of the 13th century. Or the Christ on the Cross in a group by a Tyrolian master at Innichen, Southern Tyrol, apparently carved with a blunt chopper in order to achieve a certain grotesqueness, a Christ with a regular sailor's beard— today people, imbued with the false racial ideology, would

45. Man Singing
Der singende Mann
Bronze

46. Memorial for the Dead
of World War I
*Ehrenmal fuer die Toten
des ersten Weltkriegs*
Wood

47. Detail of
Plate 46

spit at this face as something "negroid"—our unknown masters, if they worked today, could not get commissions and earn their daily bread.

Kinship to Gothic sculpture is particularly noticeable in Barlach's concealment of the body under loose clothing. (Like the pre-Renaissance masters he allowed the body to appear only when treating the theme of Christ on the Cross.) Thus, his burden of expression is borne mostly by face and hands. Barlach even went so far as to shroud a whole figure—except for a pair of bony hands—in a thick cloak. Also, a figure by Barlach rarely has a finished back; it is conceived in the Gothic fashion as standing against a wall or pillar, or in a niche.

Yet Barlach in his severity is perhaps closer to Romanesque than to Gothic sculptors. For the latter created a succession of peaks and valleys, abrupt switches from strong light to dark shadows; by vehement gestures and undulating garments they produced commotion and unrest. Barlach avoided these pictorial effects that tended to weaken the sculptural mass. His rigid simplifications compel the light to spread more evenly over the object. In his treatment of face, body and garment he is far less naturalistic than the Gothic masters.

A carving of his, strongly silhouetted as a rule, does not invite concentration on a small detail, since every part is essentially linked with an adjoining part and through it with the total structure. Though a larger work may be made of two or more pieces of wood fitted together, the impression is invariably that of a solid block hewn out of a big tree. The figure rests heavily on a base that is always included in the original concept. The neck is often short, and in most figures the arms cling tightly to the body. There is movement; yet, with the exception of a few pieces such as *Der Raecher* (The Avenger), who convulsively charges forward, or the equally aggressive *Berserker* (The Frenzied One), it is inner movement, the kinetic interplay of planes rather than bodily gesture.

In 1907 Barlach made his first wood carving, *Sitzender Steppenhirt,* the seated figure of a bearded Russian shepherd, with a mantle loosely hanging around him. He remained obsessed with wood as a medium to the end. In size these carvings—close to a hundred of them—range from pieces only a few inches high to the gigantic war memorial of Magdeburg with a height of more than eight feet. (While in this memorial the six figures appear tightly integrated on a high pedestal, in the *Frieze of Listeners* the nine very slender figures form a unit through the master's intention only rather than through physical proximity.)

Among several versions of a work the one in wood conveys to us more readily than the ones in other media the substance of the artist's spirit. But whatever medium he used, his mature works have, structurally, a common denominator: a logical, "abstract" architecture.[41] Although unconnected with the Cubists, he knew as well as they (and as all good sculptors of all periods have known intuitively) how to combine cubes, spheres, cylinders and other stereometrical bodies into aesthetically satisfying single figures or groups. He has, besides, an affinity to a painter to whom the Cubists were indebted—Paul Cézanne, whose work he admired. The two men also resembled each other in their solitary ways and carelessness of appearance; both developed slowly, and neither enjoyed an early success.

Without being consciously preoccupied by "the cylinder, the sphere, the cone" (Cézanne's "formula"), Barlach in his three-dimensional media achieved the same solidity that the painter had created on canvas. *Madame Cézanne,* in various versions, has the appearance of a peasant fashioned by Barlach. Monumentality is often conjured up by Cézanne in a tiny water-color sketch, and by Barlach in a sculpture only a few inches high. From the "concrete study of Nature" (Cézanne's words) both men went on to a grasp of form that in its vitality and sensitivity went far beyond Naturalism. Barlach wrote about himself that he had unfolded "with the devout faith of a plant." Cézanne could have said this of himself. They had in common their dislike of academic formulae and of the haziness and vagueness into which (they felt) Impressionism had finally deteriorated.

In their philosophy of life, however, they were miles apart. As

48. Façade,
St. Catherine's Church,
Luebeck, Germany

49. The Crippled Beggar
Bettler auf Kruecken
Vitrified clay

50. The Doubter
Der Zweifler
Bronze

51. Singing Acolyte
Singender Klosterschueler
Wood

he grew older, Cézanne turned into a self-centered misanthrope. (He stayed away from his mother's funeral because he would not sacrifice a day's work!) Cézanne could be entirely absorbed in painting a shirt front; to him a group of Provençal peasants required a treatment no different from a group of apples. Whatever ideas about life and death, love, sickness, greed, hunger, poverty, God and Eternal Life he may have had, he did not make them explicit in his work. The same might be said of the men who claimed to be Cézanne's legitimate heirs, the Cubists, whether they were painters or sculptors. Their near-abstract bathers, sailors, harlequins, guitar players and acrobats reveal precious little about man's anguish, about a world in turmoil.[42]

Barlach was of course aware that noble sentiments alone do not create valid art. The things he produced might appear slightly mawkish to the post-Barlach generation, which has a remarkably low tolerance for what is too often and too easily dismissed as "sentimentality." Yet even his most "sentimental" works are generally redeemed by his craftsmanship, whether he made heavy, earth-bound figures or, as in his later years, attenuated and ascetic vertical forms. They are all solid, self-contained objects, direct in deportment, firm to the grasp, devoid of unnecessary detail, static in appearance, yet flowing with inner movement—authentic sculpture.

As a rule he created single figures. They are the epitome of real men and women: they are mostly old, blind, crippled, ailing, terror-stricken, suffering from loneliness, from doubt, as most of us are at one time or another. Men, he seems to say, are doomed to live apart, and each must bear separately his burden of destiny. But they can be united by faith, like the two monks reading a book resting on their knees, or like Christ who embraces Thomas; by fear, like the two men who look up panic-stricken as if at an apparition in the sky; or by love, like the Madonna and her dead Son, who rests across her body, forming the image of a cross. "I have to be able to feel pity," he wrote. ". . . My artistic language is the human figure. . . . Man and his gesture tell enough."

52. Sketch for Memorial
for the Dead of World War I
Entwurf fuer Ehrenmal
fuer die Toten
des ersten Weltkriegs
Plaster

*In Barlach, we have a very religious type of expression: not only reli-
gious in accepted meaning, but also in the respect and interpretation
of the medium.*

The American sculptor, William Zorach

The first mention of Barlach in American letters appears to be
in an illustrated article on modern German lithographs, published in the *Print Collector's Quarterly* as early as 1913, a time
when Barlach was not widely known even in Germany. The
writer, Martin Birnbaum, owner of an avant-garde gallery in
New York City, hailed him as "one of the most original figures of
the day," and in the following year included five lithographs from
the cycle *Der tote Tag* in a show of original graphic works by
contemporary Germans. In the catalogue Barlach was intro-
duced as a "woodcarver who is like a powerful Gothic shade come
to life."

In 1924 the readers of *The Dial,* a periodical of the highest
literary standards, learned through its German correspondent,
no less a figure than Thomas Mann, that Barlach was an important dramatist. Three years later the *Germanic Review,* issued
by the German Department of Columbia University, contained a
lengthy essay on the plays Barlach had published. In 1929 the
Berlin correspondent of *The Christian Science Monitor* wrote a
perceptive note on the artist who sought "the evidence of the
inner man" rather than the representation of the forms of nature.

54. Jolly Peg-Leg
Vergnuegtes Einbein
Bronze

55. The Flute Player
Der Floetenblaeser
Bronze

In 1930 a writer commenting in *Art News* about the show of bronzes by Barlach displayed at the gallery of Flechtheim, Berlin, remarked that the "warm and living quality of wood" was "better suited to Barlach's temperament and characteristic technique."

Alfred H. Barr, Jr., in a catalogue introducing several German artists whose works were exhibited at the Museum of Modern Art in 1931, also hailed Barlach as a "carver of wood inspired by Gothic wood sculpture," though the show included his bronzes only. It was in the thirties that Barlach had a spell of fame in the United States. The economic upheaval and the news of racial persecution in Germany, of Civil War in Spain and bloody political purges in Russia caused many Americans to abandon the naïve optimism and cheerfulness that had prevailed in the "Flaming Twenties." Suddenly aware of the impossibility of having eternal, unchallenged happiness on earth, many began a reappraisal of their world. Thus it was in the America of Franklin D. Roosevelt that Barlach's reputation began to strike deeper roots. Refugees from Germany brought with them works by Barlach and spread news about him as a victim of Fascism.[43] At a time when President Roosevelt at the dedication of the new building of the Museum of Modern Art broadcast a sharp condemnation of the restriction of freedom in Germany (". . . a world turned into a stereotype, a society converted into a regiment, a life translated into a routine. . . . Crush freedom in art, and you crush art as well . . .") some of his listeners may have thought of the martyr of Guestrow who had died only recently.

Gone was the generation that demanded white marble and classical idealization. The large public monuments that with technical skill but little introspection had tried to transform prominent Americans into Roman emperors were no longer admired. American "Social Realists" of the thirties saw a spiritual brother in the German sculptor whose heart was filled with compassion for afflicted mankind. Such kinship was also based on aesthetic parallels. Had they been asked to choose between their compatriot Gutzon Borglum, who had mutilated a mountain side by arrogantly carving into it the heads of American presidents, and

56. The Reader
Der Buchleser
Bronze

57. Shivering Old Woma[n]
Frierende A[lte]
Bron[ze]

the humbler, more passionate Barlach, they would not have hesitated to decide for the German.[44]

America's young sculptors came to admire Barlach's skill in wood carving, to share his preference for the Gothic over the Renaissance, and to agree with the critic who had praised Barlach's work for the absence of what he called a "self-conscious effort for virtuoso distinction." As wood—a medium particularly suited to a democratic society—became more popular on this side of the Atlantic, Americans began to study, first with curiosity and then with reverence, the work of this artist who distilled an endless variety of human passions from his medium. One might find poetic justice in the fact that while Barlach's death had been passed over in silence in his native country, long obituaries appeared in the American press. In the fall of 1938 the Buchholz Gallery, transferred from Berlin to the more hospitable New York, held a Memorial Exhibition. The catalogue paid him homage: "With the passing of Ernst Barlach on October twenty-fourth, the world lost one of the finest sculptors."

After the United States had entered World War II, the Buchholz Gallery continued to show works by this German anti-Nazi. Individual pieces by Barlach were also on view at the Museum of Modern Art; for instance, in a "Free Art" exhibition arranged here in 1942.[45] But after the war interest in Barlach and his art began to dwindle. To the young artists who were just emerging, Barlach with his often heavy, usually static forms and his messianic fervor suddenly seemed rather "old-fashioned." For the sculptural quality of weight, a *sine qua non* in traditional work, had given way to other qualities, to mobiles, to attenuated forms rhythmically moving through space. Wood and bronze were replaced by iron, steel and other metals: bent, hammered, welded or annealed with uninhibited freedom. Plastics, synthetic stone, discarded farm equipment, bits of furniture and other novel materials took the place of more conventional media.

The young artists were, of course, absolutely justified in trying out new methods, new approaches, new materials. They and the critics who supported them were wrong, however, in judging

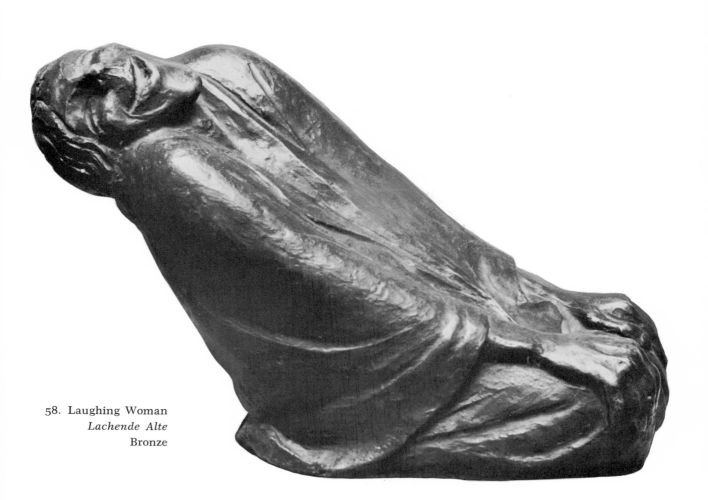

58. Laughing Woman
Lachende Alte
Bronze

the work of a man born nearly a hundred years earlier by the aesthetic yardsticks of an era of space flights and of nuclear fission. If Barlach actually is too "clumsily soulful" for the "cool" new generation, then the medieval carvings or the Rembrandts which he so admired are also *passé*. If the only acceptable mode of expression today is the abstract, then the artists whose works were assembled by the Museum of Modern Art in 1959 for the "New Images of Man" exhibition are also out of step with the times.[46]

Actually, terms like "modern" and "old-fashioned" have little

59. Frieze of Listeners
Fries der Lauschenden
Wood

merit. Only an artist's honesty, wisdom and skill matter.[47] Barlach was one of the last important artists to produce easily recognizable images, and he may have exhausted the possibilities of the monolithic block. Yet he succeeded in being inventive within conventions established by a five-thousand-year-old tradition, and he sought no more. The German Expressionist painters had goals similar to Barlach's: their common concern was, as Barlach said of himself, "what man can suffer and must suffer."

It is interesting that in England, which suffered so terribly in the war and was so slow in making an economic recovery, Barlach has had a better press than in the more prosperous and relatively unscathed United States. The response to the Barlach shows seen here in the 1950's and 1960's generally wavered between mild enthusiasm and polite rejection. By contrast, England's only Barlach show—at the Arts Council Galleries, London, in 1961—was favorably received. "What Barlach achieved and the early Gothic visionaries just failed to achieve, is human dignity," Eric Newton wrote in *Time and Tide*. "The boy who clasps his knee, leans back and bursts into song is a more serious musician and is producing a more complex melody than any chorister. The little double statue of the meeting between Christ and Saint Thomas is more moving than any Gothic visitation." Barlach would have agreed that human dignity was his goal, but he would have blushed at the idea that his own work might possibly be superior to that of any Gothic masters.

And Nikolaus Pevsner commented with indignation in *The Listener*: "If, for reasons of the violent but imprecise impacts of the abstract artists of today, those who care for art in this country have lost their appreciation of Van Gogh's 'Potato Eaters' and consequently are unable to appreciate Barlach's 'Beggars'—in that case I can only say goodbye."

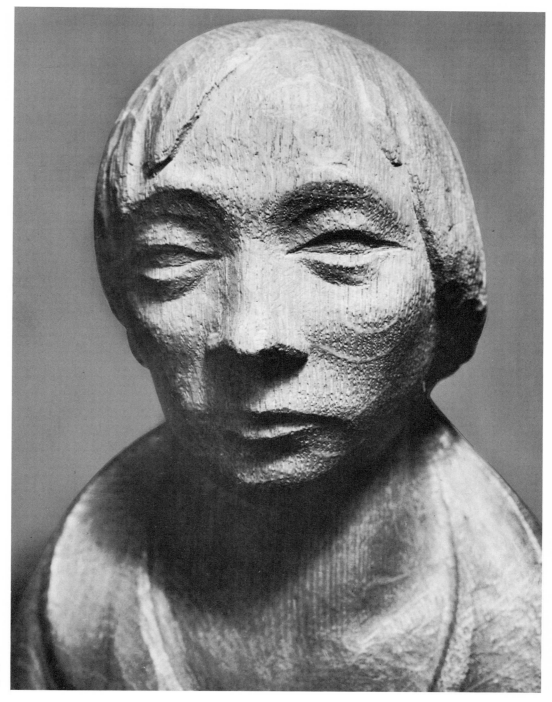

60. Detail of Plate 59:
The Sensitive Man
Der Empfindsame

61. Detail of Plate 59
The Believer
Der Glaeubige

62. Detail of Plate 59:
The Expectant Woman
Die Erwartende

63. Detail of
Plate 59:
The Blind
Der Blinde

64. Detail of
Plate 59:
The Dancer
Die Taenzerin

65. Detail of Plate 59:
The Wanderer
Der Wanderer

66. Detail of Plate 59:
The Dreaming Woman
Die Traeumende

67. Detail of Plate 59:
The Blessed Man
Der Begnadete

68. Detail of Plate 59:
The Pilgrim Woman
Die Pilgerin

69. Youth
Jugend
Colored pencil

70. Russian Peasant
Russischer Bauer
Charcoal

71. Russian Village L
Russiches Dorfleb
Pen and ink and br

72. Russian Courtship · *Russisches Liebeswerben* · Pencil

73. Frost and Hunger · *Frost und Hunger* · Charcoal

74. Kneeling Wor
Kniende F
Char

75. Malicious Gossi
Klatschhexen
Charcoal and ink

76. Sketch for The Dead Day · *Skizze fuer Der tote Tag* · Charcoal or chalk with ink

77. Sketch for The Poor Cousin
Skizze fuer Der arme Vetter
Charcoal

78. Defensive One · *Abwehrender* · Charcoal

80. Woman
Frau
Charcoal

81. Man and Girl
Mann und Maedchen
Charcoal

82. Old Woman on Crutches
Alte Frau auf Kruecken
Chracoal

83. A Mother's Happiness · *Mutterglueck* · Lithogaph

84. Woman at the Hearth
   Dir Frau am Herd
   Lithograph

85. Woman Falling
Stuerzende Frau
Lithograph

Aus einem neuzeitlichen Totentanz·

86. From a Modern
Dance of Death
*Aus einem neuzeitlichen
Totentanz*
Lithograph

87. Star Gazer II
Sterndeuter II
Lithograph

88. Mors Imperator
    Woodcut

89. Child's Grave
Kindertod
Woodcut

90. Grave Robbers
Kreuz-und Sargraeuber
Woodcut

91. Group in a Storm
Gruppe im Sturm
Woodcut

92. **The First Day**
Der erste Tag
Woodcut

93. **The Cathedrals**
Die Dome
Woodcut

95. Traveling Death
Wandernder Tod
Lithograph

94. Dance of Death II
Totentanz II
Woodcut

155

96. Erl King
Erlkoenig
Lithograph

97. Schiller's Ode to Joy
Schiller's *An die Freude*
Woodcut

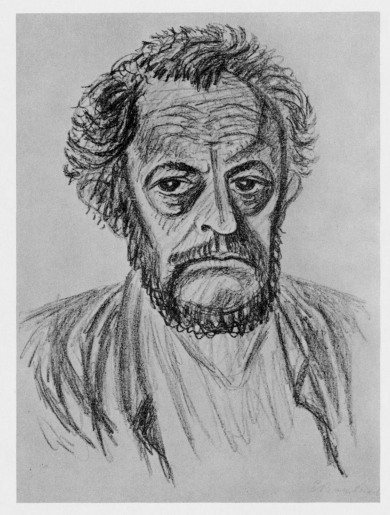

98. Self Portrait
Selbstbildnis
Lithograph

99. Hope and Despair
Hoffnung und Verzweiflung
Lithograph

100. The New Day · *Der neue Tag* · Lithograph

SCULPTURE

1. Russian Beggar Woman (*Russische Bettlerin*)
   1906 · Ceramic · 11 inches
   Konstmuseum, Goeteborg, Sweden

2. The Melon Eater (*Der Melonenesser*)
   1907 · Bronze · 13¼ inches
   Wallraf-Richartz Museum, Cologne

3. Russian Beggar Woman (*Russische Bettlerin*)
   1907 · Ceramic · 6 inches
   Behn-Haus, Luebeck, Germany

4. Beggar Woman with Child (*Bettlerin mit Kind*)
   1907 · Plaster · 14 inches
   Collection Mr. and Mrs. M. A. Lipschultz, Chicago

5. Seated Peasant Woman (*Sitzende Baeuerin*)
   1908 · Porcelain · 9 inches
   Busch-Reisinger Museum, Harvard University,
       Cambridge, Massachusetts

6. Russian Lovers (*Russisches Liebespaar*)
   1908 · Porcelain · 8 inches
   Barlach-Haus, Hamburg

7. Shepherd in a Storm (*Schaefer im Sturm*)
   1908 · Wood · 20 inches
   Kunsthalle, Bremen

8. Man Berserk (*Der Berserker*)
   1910 · Bronze · 21½ inches
   Barlach-Haus, Hamburg

9. Lonely Man (*Der Einsame*)
   1911 · Bronze · 23¼ inches
   Collection Erich Cohn, New York
   Photo courtesy Galerie St. Etienne, New York

10. Man Drawing a Sword (*Der Schwertzieher*)
    1911 · Wood · 29¾ inches
    Cranbrook Academy of Art, Bloomfield Hills, Michigan

11. The Vision (*Die Vision*)
    1912 · Wood
    Lower Section 15¾ inches, Upper Section 31 inches
    Galerie des 20. Jahrhunderts, Berlin-Charlottenburg

12. The Walker (*Der Spaziergaenger*)
    1912 · Bronze · 20 inches
    Collection Erich Cohn, New York
    Photo courtesy Galerie St. Etienne, New York

13. Panic Fright (*Panischer Schrecken*)
    1912 · Wood · 24½ inches
    Collection G. Luetgens, Kuesnacht-Zurich

14. The Abandoned Ones (*Die Verlassenen*)
   1913 · Wood · 52 inches
   National-Galerie, Staatliche Museen, Berlin-East

15. Migrants (*Wandersleute*)
   1913 · Wood · 21¾ inches
   Collection George P. F. Katz, Great Neck, New York

16. The Village Fiddler (*Der Dorfgeiger*)
   1914 · Wood · 24¾ inches
   Private Collection, New York
   Photo courtesy Galerie St. Etienne, New York

17. The Avenger (*Der Raecher*)
   1914 · Bronze · 17¼ inches
   Collection Mr. and Mrs. Norbert Schimmel, Great Neck, New York
   Photo courtesy Galerie St. Etienne, New York

18. The Ecstatic One (*Der Ekstatiker*)
   1916 · Wood · 20½ inches
   Kunsthaus, Zurich

19. Freezing Girl (*Frierendes Maedchen*)
   1917 · Wood · 29¼ inches
   Barlach-Haus, Hamburg

20. The Man Pilloried (*Der Mann im Stock*)
   1918 · Wood · 29 inches
   Kunsthalle, Hamburg

21. The Law Giver, also called Moses (*Der Gesetzgeber, auch Moses benannt*)
   1919 · Wood · 72¾ inches
   Barlach-Haus, Hamburg

22. Detail of Plate 21

23. Hooded Beggar Woman (*Verhuellte Bettlerin*)
   1919 · Wood · 15 inches
   Private Collection, New York
   Photo courtesy Galerie St. Etienne, New York

24. The Blind Man Carrying the Halt (*Der Blinde traegt den Lahmen*)
   1919 · Clay · 21½ inches
   Kunsthalle, Bremen

25. Ecstatic Woman (*Ekstatische Frau*)
   1920 · Bronze · 14½ inches
   Photo courtesy Weyhe Gallery, New York

26. Old Woman Dancing (*Tanzende Alte*)
   1920 · Bronze · 19¼ inches
   Collection Mr. and Mrs. Kurt H. Grunebaum, Harrison, New York
   Photo courtesy Galerie St. Etienne, New York

27. The Fugitive (*Der Fluechtling*)
   1920 · Bronze · 14 inches
   Photo courtesy Curt Valentin, New York

28. The Procuress II (*Die Kupplerin II*)
    1920 · Bronze · 18¼ inches
    Kunsthalle, Mannheim, Germany

29. Old Woman with a Flask (*Die Alte mit der Flasche*)
    1920 · Clay · 9¼ inches
    Barlach Estate, Guestrow, Germany

30. Standing Peasant Woman (*Stehende Baeuerin*)
    1921 · Wood · 38 inches
    Collection Fritz Niescher, Aachen, Germany

31. Detail of Plate 30

32. The Young Woman (*Das junge Weib*)
    1922 · Wood · 39½ inches
    Frank M. Hall Collection, University of Nebraska, Lincoln, Nebraska

33. Cloaked Man (*Mann mit dem Mantel*)
    1922 · Wood · 31½ inches
    Bayrische Gemaeldesammlungen, Munich

34. God the Father Hovering (*Schwebender Gottvater*)
    1922 · Terra cotta · 20 inches
    Collection Mr. and Mrs. Kurt H. Grunebaum, Harrison, New York
    Photo courtesy Galerie St. Etienne, New York

35. Sleeping Pair (*Zwei Schlafende*)
    1923 · Wood · 29 inches
    Museum Folkwang, Essen

36. Detail of Plate 35

37. Horror (*Das Grauen*)
    1923 · Wood · 35¼ inches
    Museum Folkwang, Essen

38. Pregnant Girl (*Schwangeres Maedchen*)
    1924 · Wood · 34½ inches
    Nathan Collection, New York
    Photo courtesy Galerie St. Etienne, New York

39. Group of three Figures, also called Death (*Gruppe aus drei Figuren, auch Der Tod*)
    1925 · Bronze · 13½ inches
    Barlach-Haus, Hamburg

40. The Reunion, also called Christ and Thomas (*Das Wiedersehen, auch Christus und Thomas benannt*)
    1926 · Bronze · 19 inches
    Collection Erich Cohn, New York
    Photo courtesy Galerie St. Etienne, New York

41. Detail of Plate 40

42. Head of the Guestrow Memorial (*Kopf des Ehrenmals*)
    1927 · Bronze · 14 inches
    Museum of Modern Art, New York

58. Laughing Woman (*Lachende Alte*)
1937 · Bronze · 8⅛ inches
Collection Joseph H. Hirshhorn, New York

59. Frieze of Listeners (*Fries der Lauschenden*)
1930–1935 · Wood · 43 inches
Barlach-Haus, Hamburg

60. Detail of Figure 59: The Sensitive Man (*Der Empfindsame*)

61. Detail of Figure 59: The Believer (*Der Glaeubige*)

62. Detail of Figure 59: The Expectant Woman (*Die Erwartende*)

63. Detail of Figure 59: The Blind Man (*Der Blinde*)

64. Detail of Figure 59: The Dancer (*Die Taenzerin*)

65. Detail of Figure 59: The Wanderer (*Der Wanderer*)

66. Detail of Figure 59: The Dreaming Woman (*Die Traeumende*)

67. Detail of Figure 59: The Blessed Man (*Der Begnadete*)

68. Detail of Figure 59: The Pilgrim Woman (*Die Pilgerin*)

DRAWINGS

69. Youth (*Jugend*)
Date unknown · Colored pencil · 9 x 6 inches
Kunsthalle, Hamburg

70. Russian Peasant (*Russischer Bauer*)
1906 · Charcoal
Barlach Estate, Guestrow, Germany

71. Russian Village Life (*Russisches Dorfleben*)
C. 1907 · Pen and ink and brush · 22¾ x 18 inches
Barlach-Haus, Hamburg

72. Russian Courtship (*Russisches Liebeswerben*)
1907 · Pencil · 17½ x 25 inches
Collection Henry M. Roland, London

73. Frost and Hunger (*Frost und Hunger*)
Date unknown · Charcoal · 18 x 22¾ inches
Kunsthalle, Mannheim, Germany

74. Kneeling Woman (*Kniende Frau*)
Date unknown · Charcoal
Barlach Estate, Guestrow, Germany

75. Malicious Gossips (*Klatschhexen*)
Date unknown · Charcoal and ink · 11 x 15 inches
Collection F. G. von Stockert, Frankfort on the Main

76. Sketch for The Dead Day (Skizze fuer *Der tote Tag*)
C. 1912 · Charcoal or chalk with ink · 10⅝ x 13⅛ inches
Dial Collection, anonymous loan to Worcester Museum, Worcester, Massachusetts

77. Sketch for The Poor Cousin (Skizze fuer *Der arme Vetter*)
1918 · Charcoal
Barlach Estate, Guestrow, Germany

78. Defensive One (*Abwehrender*)
    1920 · Charcoal · 9 x 12 inches
    Barlach Estate, Guestrow, Germany

79. Despair (*Verzweiflung*)
    1922 · Charcoal
    Collection Fritz Niescher, Aachen, Germany

80. Woman (*Frau*)
    1923 · Charcoal
    Barlach Estate, Guestrow, Germany

81. Man and Girl (*Mann und Maedchen*)
    Date unknown · Charcoal · 12½ x 5½ inches
    Collection Mr. and Mrs. Norbert Schimmel, Great Neck, New York
    Photo courtesy Galerie St. Etienne, New York

82. Old Woman on Crutches (*Alte Frau auf Kruecken*)
    Date unknown · Charcoal · 11¾ x 9 inches
    Collection George P. F. Katz, Great Neck, New York

PRINTS

83. A Mother's Happiness (*Mutterglueck*)
    1904/05 · Lithograph · 9 x 11 inches
    Kunsthalle, Hamburg

84. Woman at the Hearth (*Die Frau am Herd*)
    Scene from The Dead Day (*Szene aus Der tote Tag*)
    1910/11 · Lithograph · 10 x 12¾ inches
    Yale University Art Gallery, New Haven, Connecticut

85. Woman Falling (*Stuerzende Frau*)
    Scene from The Dead Day (*Szene aus Der tote Tag*)
    1910/11 · Lithograph · 11 x 12½ inches
    Kunsthalle, Hamburg

86. From a Modern Dance of Death (*Aus einem neuzeitlichen Totentanz*)
    1916 · Lithograph · 12 x 8 inches
    Kunsthalle, Hamburg

87. Star Gazer II (*Sterndeuter II*)
    1916/17 · Lithograph · 20 x 27 inches
    Kunsthalle, Hamburg

88. Mors Imperator
    1919 · Woodcut · 10¾ x 14¼ inches
    Courtesy Inter Nationes, Bonn

89. Child's Grave (*Kindertod*)
    1919 · Woodcut · 9⅜ x 14 3/16 inches
    Dial Collection, Worcester Art Museum, Worcester, Massachusetts

90. Grave Robbers (*Kreuz— und Sargraeuber*)
    1919 · Woodcut · 16¼ x 14¼ inches
    Yale University Art Gallery, New Haven, Connecticut

91. Group in a Storm (*Gruppe im Sturm*)
   1919 · Woodcut · 7 x 5½ inches
   Museum of Modern Art, New York

92. The First Day (*Der erste Tag*)
   From The Transformations of God (Aus *Die Wandlungen Gottes*)
   1920 · Woodcut · 10 x 14 inches
   Courtesy Weyhe Gallery, New York

93. The Cathedrals (*Die Dome*)
   From The Transformations of God (Aus *Die Wandlungen Gottes*)
   1920 · Woodcut · 12⅞ x 17¾ inches
   Museum of Modern Art, New York

94. Dance of Death II (*Totentanz II*)
   From The Transformations of God (Aus *Die Wandlungen Gottes*)
   1921 · Woodcut · 9⅞ x 14 inches
   Barlach-Gesellschaft, Hamburg

95. Traveling Death (*Wandernder Tod*)
   1923 · Lithograph · 10⅝ x 13½ inches
   Museum of Modern Art, New York

96. Erl King (*Erlkoenig*)
   From Goethe's Poems (Aus *Goethe: Gedichte*)
   1924 · 10 x 8 inches · Lithograph
   Kunsthalle, Hamburg

97. Schiller's Ode to Joy (Schiller's *An die Freude*)
   1924 · Woodcut · 10 x 14 inches
   Courtesy Weyhe Gallery, New York

98. Self Portrait (*Selbstbildnis*)
   1928 · Lithograph · 17½ x 12 inches
   Frank M. Hall Collection, University of Nebraska Art Galleries, Lincoln

99. Hope and Despair (*Hoffnung und Verzweiflung*)
   1931 · Lithograph · 12¾ x 18⅛ inches
   Yale University Art Gallery, New Haven, Connecticut

100. The New Day (*Der neue Tag*)
   1932 · Lithograph · 12½ x 17 inches
   Kunsthalle, Hamburg

Notes

1. By now it is irrelevant who was the first to use the term "Expressionist" or "Expressionism." Was it Henri Matisse? The British writer Roger Fry? The German art historian Wilhelm Worringer? There is no doubt that by 1911 it had become part of art jargon. A reviewer of works by the French *Fauves* in *Der Cicerone* (Berlin) observed: "They no longer want to reproduce an impression which they gain from nature, that is to say, paint naturalistically, but they want to express

the impression which their observation exercises on their artistic imagination."

This definition is rather vague: where is the artist who does not aim at expressing the impact of a vision upon his imagination? Formally, an Expressionist work might be recognized by the spontaneous, free distortion or exaggeration of the ordinary forms and colors in nature. Philosophically, it indicates predominant emphasis on feeling, intuition, imagination. Socially, it stands for revolt against any sort of hypocrisy—ethical, moral or political—sanctioned by the older order. As the German art historian and museum director Ludwig Justi put it, Expressionism was a "revelation of the profoundly problematic conditions of Europe at the turn of the century." Barlach, whose major work was done after 1906, certainly belongs to the period of Expressionism which reached its climax in the first years of the Weimar Republic.

2. In *Weltanschauung* Barlach was akin to Kollwitz, who wrote in her diary in the middle of World War I: "Humanity's goal goes beyond the first stage of happiness—elimination of poverty, disease—also beyond the complete development of the forces within itself. The goal is to develop divinity, spirituality." (*Diaries and Letters of Kaethe Kollwitz*, Chicago, 1955.)

3. The modest Barlach did not like being called a "Godseeker." To an interviewer for a Danish newspaper in 1932 he declared:

I desire nothing except to be an artist pure and simple. It is my belief that what cannot be expressed in words can, through plastic form, reach another man's soul. To be sure, it is the pleasure of my creative urge to hover again and again over such problems as the meaning of life and other mountain peaks in the realm of the spirit.

But, he added, he had no intention

to preach, to present solutions, to hand out tags defining Good and Evil—in a word to do anything at all except to make forms emerge out of the mystery of Existence, forms that are credible and that take along with them no more of me than I am allowed to give them. . . ."

4. In November 1938, the mayor of Wedel asked the *Reichsminister fuer Volksaufklaerung und Propaganda* for permission to place a memorial tablet on the house where the late Barlach had been born. He was told that this was not "desirable." While Goebbels' representative conceded that Barlach had artistic talent, his art had to be characterized as "volksfremd" (alien to the German people). Moreover, he had "deeply wounded German popular sentiment through his war memorial at Magdeburg." A tablet was finally affixed to the house in January 1946.

5. One of his quick Parisian sketches contains the likeness of Lautrec's friend and patron, the singer and café owner Aristide Bruant, one of the most colorful figures of Montmartre.

6. Later, Barlach expressed dislike of Rodin's work, except for the *Balzac*.

7. Mecklenburg is today part of the German Democratic Republic (Communist East Germany) and not easily accessible to Western visitors. The original Teutonic inhabitants were overrun in the sixth century

by Slavic tribes, and to this day many rural Mecklenburgers have the Slavic cast of feature so often seen in Barlach's figures.

Guestrow is in the larger of the two historic duchies comprising Mecklenburg. The region, washed by the Baltic Sea, is flat. There are large expanses of marshy moors, sprawling pastures, and many rivers and lakes. The winters are severe.

8. One of the deeply stirring lithographs is entitled *Pax dona nobis* (Give us peace).

9. In 1918 he received his only commission from the Imperial Government—to fashion a memorial for a military cemetery. It was never executed, as the government fell soon after, but the original concept of a crucifixion ultimately was adapted for the Elizabeth Church at Marburg in 1931.

10. A conservative German artist called Barlach's war memorial for Magdeburg a "disgrace to Germany," and in the periodical *Theologie der Gegenwart* Barlach was accused of lacking "reverence before God."

11. One of his arch enemies was the fanatically anti-Semitic literary historian, Adolf Bartels, who as early as 1926 had convinced himself, and perhaps some of his readers also, that Barlach was Jewish and therefore unacceptable.

12. Even before Hitler's usurpation of power, Nazis for a short time ruled the government in the state of Thuringia. One of their official actions was to eliminate Barlach's works, along with those of other Expressionists, from the Schlossmuseum in Weimar.

13. Even so eminent a museum director as Berlin's Wilhelm von Bode decried what he called the "form-lacking creations by Barlach which sit on the ground like sacks of flour."

14. Created by Frederick the Great as the highest order Prussia could award for military services, the *Pour le Mérite* after 1842 was also awarded for distinction in the arts and sciences.

15. The advice he gave his cousin Karl and other trusted people—to join the Nazi party—has been misinterpreted and misunderstood: he hoped they could undermine the Party from within by their idealism. This was a remedy conceived in sheer desperation.

16. On March 22, 1933, upon learning of the establishment of concentration camps, he scratched into a clay relief, *Die Vision* (The Vision), made many years earlier, the words, "*Freiheit, die ich meine.*" This is the opening line of a poem by Max von Schenkendorf, a paean to freedom written when Germany was under the yoke of Napoleon.

17. The Magdeburg Memorial was moved to a cellar in the Kronprinzenpalais in Berlin, where Kaethe Kollwitz saw it in 1936. She wrote: "I knew it only from a reproduction. It is as good as I had thought from the reproduction, in fact better. There the war experience of 1914–1918 has really been fixed. Impossible for adherents of the Third Reich, of course, but for me and many others it is *true*. When you look from one figure to the others—this silence. Where mouths are ordinarily made for speaking—here they are shut so firmly, as though they

have never laughed. But he drew a drape over the mother's head. Good, Barlach!"

18. *Art under a Dictatorship*, New York, 1954.

19. After the "purge" of 1937 only one sculpture by Barlach remained on view in a public collection: the *Schaefer im Sturm* (Shepherd in a Storm), a wood carving of 1908, at the Kunsthalle in Bremen.

    In June 1939 works by Barlach, confiscated from German museums, along with other "degenerate" art, were put up for auction at the Galerie Fischer in Lucerne, Switzerland, to yield the Reich urgently needed foreign currency.

20. Fearing prosecution for his collaboration with the Nazis, Boehmer committed suicide at the end of World War II.

21. The pencil sketch she made of Barlach on his bier has survived. Referring to this sketch, the American art historian Bernard S. Myers wrote: "What greater moment of pity could be envisioned than her drawing of the proscribed sculptor Ernst Barlach on his deathbed . . . what more dematerialized symbol of the disappearance of the body and the survival of the spirit?" (*The German Expressionists*, New York, 1957.)

22. Julius Rupp, leader of Germany's Free Religious Congregation, was Kollwitz's maternal grandfather.

23. At the funeral in Ratzeburg, Barlach's lifelong friend, Friedrich Duesel, declared: "Powerful and lofty, touching and shattering though his works are, more beautiful and more noble still, were his heart, his soul."

24. The Nazi Party sent 1500 Reichsmark to the congregation in Guestrow, a small sum—the price of the metal as melted down for munitions.

25. At the twenty-fifth Biennale of Venice (1950) in the German section sculptures and drawings by Barlach were abundantly represented.

26. The *Mater Dolorosa* in the St. Nikolaus Church, Kiel, was destroyed in World War II along with the church itself. The Crucifix of Marburg survived, and replicas are now in a church in Bremen and in the cathedral of Guestrow.

    The Protestant parish in Cologne bought the surviving cast of the Angel of Guestrow, and placed it in the east apse of the Antonite Church. A new cast was made from it for the Guestrow cathedral where it was installed in the south nave.

    Barlach's three figures were finally installed in niches on the façade of the St. Catherine Church in 1947. Realizing the slight chance that he would live to see the downfall of the Nazi regime, the aged Barlach expressed the wish that the project would be completed by a much younger man, his colleague Gerhard Marcks. Marcks, indeed, was able after the war to add six sculptures of his own to the three made by Barlach.

27. One of his initial literary efforts, the story *Willy der Sumpfmaler* (Willy the Swamp Painter), appeared in an issue of *Dresdener Zeitung* as early as 1891.

28. *Die weissen Blaetter. Eine Monatsschrift,* a monthly published by Paul Cassirer, Berlin.

29. *The Modern German Drama,* New York, 1963.

30. *The Theatre of the Absurd,* New York, 1961.

31. Some of the earliest *Simplizissimus* drawings were made after clay models. One may recall that Daumier, too, made clay models instead of pencil sketches to aid him in the production of graphic art.

32. See Claus Virch, *Ernst Barlachs Entwuerfe zum Kieler Geistkaempfer,* Kiel, 1953.

33. An expanded edition of *Zeichnungen,* with a revised version of the original preface by Paul Fechter, was issued by R. Piper Verlag in 1948 on the tenth anniversary of the artist's death.

34. What Ernst Ludwig Kirchner, the most prolific of all modern German printmakers, wrote about the print in general can be applied with particular emphasis to the woodcut: "The very technical manipulations release in the artist powers which do not come into play in the much easier handwork of drawing and painting."

35. It is significant that his early drawings are often to be seen in exhibitions of his works, while the sculptures shown rarely predate the pivotal trip to Russia.

36. Young Barlach once visited him, probably in the hope of getting employment as an assistant.

37. "Barlach's cripple and his singing girl [in the niches of St. Catherine's Church, Luebeck], typifying fundamental aspects of human sorrow and joy, respectively, submit to a divine law of life. Matter constitutes the impenetrable kernel of Barlach's sculpture. Where Lehmbruck eases the burden of weight, Barlach concentrates and condenses it. Space remains a force outside his figures—a threatening force, alien and unreachable, that plays the role of fate; man is rebellious and revolts against it, he is powerless and it destroys him; he entrusts himself to it and it carries him.

"A content so specific and determined is rare in twentieth-century sculpture and peculiar to the sculptor-poet Barlach. His concern with subject matter might occasionally have been burdensome to the formal aspects of his work had they not been saved by the intuition of the genuine sculptor. . . . Barlach chops off the ebb and flow of sculptural forms, the outward pressures from their own inner core, and superimposes a form and a formula of expression. Fortunately he was a master of his formula and knew how to vary it superbly as well as how to blend it with his respective content." Alfred Neumeyer, *The Search for Meaning in Modern Art,* Englewood Cliffs, 1964.

38. See *Plastik und Kunsthandwerk von Malern des deutschen Expressionismus,* the catalogue of an exhibition held at Schleswig and at Hamburg in 1960.

39. ". . . The closed-in, angular and compact forms that we find in the works of Barlach . . . are to be understood as a reaction against the influence of painting, as a meditation on one of the age-old fundamentals of sculpture, the rendering not of the transient, momentary

visual stimulation but of enduring and supra-personal values. Barlach's *Man Alone*, heavy, simplified forms carved in wood, portrays solitude not as a passing mood but as the lot of man. The sturdy mass of the body leaning to one side, imprisoned in its cloak, is a translation into sculptural terms of a statement concerning the nature of human existence." Eduard Trier, *Form and Space*, New York, 1961.

40. The German title of the essay is *Lob der Bodenstaendigkeit*.

41. "The bold, clear way in which Rembrandt gives an appearance of solidity to his portrait is closely related to the way Barlach conceives of the sculpture *Man Drawing a Sword*. In his painting, Rembrandt makes more emphatic the feeling of solidity we are apt to attribute to the figure because we see it as existing in pictorial space. Similarly, Barlach heightens our feeling for the solidity and mass of a figure that, because it is a piece of sculpture, we naturally see as a tangible object in real space. In the Barlach sculpture the essential characteristics of the figure are again revealed to us through the relationship of a few broad planes. The robe stretched between the legs of the figure, the breadth of this garment as it moves away from the knees, and the unbroken expanse of the cloak falling from the shoulders, all are planes that act to move our eye swiftly over the figure and to form an idea for us of a man of great strength." Bates Lowry, *The Visual Experience*, New York, 1961.

42. Barlach once uttered this stern warning: "Whosoever concerns himself with aesthetics for its own sake, does something much akin to a sin against the Holy Spirit."

See also Friedrich Nietzsche's attacks on Art for Art's Sake:

"The struggle against a purpose in art is always a struggle against the moral tendency in art, against its subordination to morality. *L'art pour l'art* means, 'Let morality go to the devil!'. . . . Art is the great stimulus to life: how can it be regarded as pointless, as *l'art pour l'art* . . .?" *The Twilight of the Idols*.

43. Jewish refugees took their beloved Barlachs with them to Palestine where, in 1940, an exhibition of these works was held at the National Bezalel Museum in Jerusalem.

44. Bronzes by Barlach can be found in many museums in the United States; the most notable of them is the *Geistkaempfer* at the Minneapolis Institute of Arts. The Busch-Reisinger Museum of Harvard, in Cambridge, Mass., owns a cast of Barlach's *Crippled Beggar* (vitrified clay), one of the figures for the St. Catherine Church in Luebeck. An important wood sculpture, *Man Drawing a Sword*, is at the Cranbrook Academy of Art, Bloomfield Hills, Michigan. A cast of the Guestrow Memorial Head is at the Museum of Modern Art, New York.

45. Between 1931 and 1944 works by Barlach were shown in the United States in the following major exhibitions:

1931. The circulating show, *Modern German Prints*, arranged by the association of German illustrators of books, of which Barlach was an honorary member.

1933. *Modern Ecclesiastic Art*, at the World's Fair in Chicago. (Barlach was on the honorary advisory board for this special exhibition.)

1936. *Modern Painters and Sculptors as Illustrators*, at the Museum of Modern Art, New York.

1938. *German Sculptors*, at the Germanic Museum (now Busch-Reisinger Museum) of Harvard University.

1939. *Contemporary German Art*, at the Institute of Modern Art, Boston; *Golden Gate Exhibition*, San Francisco, California.

1941. *Eight Sculptors and their Drawings* and *20th Century Drawing*, both at the Museum of Modern Art, New York.

1944. *Exhibition of Religious Art Today*, at the Institute of Modern Art, Boston.

46. The German-born philosopher, Paul Tillich, wrote in a preface to the catalogue:

> As in the reality of our lives, so in its mirror of the visual arts, the human protest arose against the fate to become a thing. . . . They [the new figurative artists] want to regain the image of man in their paintings and sculptures, but they are too honest to turn back to earlier naturalistic or idealistic forms.

47. Were he still alive, Barlach would have felt like Gerhard Marcks, who in 1958 wrote to his colleague, Renée Sintenis:

> We have seen so many changes in sculptural fashion and now, at last, it has passed us by. But in so doing, it has freed us from many burdens; now, in the nature of things, we can travel lightly, along the road we have chosen. . . . Isn't it a joy to stand aside from the hurly-burly of the day?

Chronology

1870	Ernst Barlach born on January 2 in the town of Wedel, Holstein, near Hamburg, eldest son of the physician Dr. Georg Barlach and his wife Louise, née Vollert.
1884	Death of Dr. Barlach.
1888–1891	Ernst Barlach is student at the School of Applied Arts, Hamburg.
1891–1895	Student at the Academy of Art in Dresden.
1895–1896	Lives in Paris, where he briefly attends the Académie Julian.
1897–1898	Altona and Hamburg.
1899–1901	Berlin.
1901–1904	Wedel. Produces small pieces of ceramics.
1904–1905	Teaches for seven months at the Trade School of Ceramics at Hoehr (Westerwald), east of the Rhine River.
1905–1906	Lives in Berlin. Son, Nikolaus, born in 1906. (The mother is a model, Rosa Limana Schwab.)

1906	August to September, journey to Southern Russia.
1907	In Berlin, signs a contract with the dealer Paul Cassirer. Becomes a member of the artists' association Die Sezession.
1909	Recipient of the Villa Romana Prize. Lives in Florence. Makes the acquaintance of the poet Theodor Daeubler.
1910	Settles permanently in the town of Guestrow, Mecklenburg, with his mother to keep house for him and his son.
1912	Publication of his first play, *Der tote Tag*.
1914–1916	Volunteer helper in a day center for soldiers' children; brief service in the reserve of the German army.
1917	First major exhibition (at the gallery of Cassirer, Berlin).
1919	Becomes a member of the Academy of Arts, Berlin.
1920	Death of mother.
1924	Awarded the Kleist Prize for his play, *Die Suendflut*.
1925	Elected Honorary Member of the Academy of Arts, Munich.
1926	Retrospective exhibition at the gallery of Cassirer.
1927	Memorial for the cathedral in Guestrow.
1928	Memorial for Kiel.
1930	On his sixtieth birthday, retrospective exhibitions in Berlin.
1932	Memorial for Hamburg.
1933	January, in a radio address defends the independence of the artist in the political upheaval of the time. February, created a Knight of the Prussian Order *Pour le Mérite*. March, with the victory of the Nazi Party, discrimination against progressive artists such as Barlach becomes the official policy of the German Reich.
1934	Memorial in Magdeburg removed.
1935	Performance of the play, *Die echten Sedemunds*, at Altona cancelled by government order.
1936	Most copies of *Zeichnungen* (a selection from Barlach's drawings) confiscated and destroyed by the Gestapo. Made honorary member of the Artists' Association, Sezession, and of the Austrian Sculptors' Association in the Academy of Fine Arts, both in Vienna.
1937	*Das Wiedersehen* included in the "Degenerate Art" exhibition at Munich. 381 works by Barlach removed from public collections in Germany. The memorial removed from the cathedral in Guestrow.
1938	Death from heart failure in a hospital at Rostock, Mecklenburg, on October 24. Burial at Ratzeburg, October 28.

The literature about Barlach—almost exclusively in German—is so large that I will confine myself to the mention of informative works that have appeared since 1945:

Barlach, Karl: *Mein Vetter Ernst Barlach*, Bremen, 1960.
Carls, C. D.: *Ernst Barlach*, Berlin, 1958.
Fechter, Paul: *Ernst Barlach*, Guetersloh, 1957.
Flemming, Willi: *Ernst Barlach*, Munich, 1958.
Franck, Hans: *Barlach, Leben und Werk*, Stuttgart, 1961.
Schurek, Paul: *Begegnungen mit Barlach*, Berlin, 1960.

Of the *catalogue raisonné* of Barlach's work, two volumes edited by Friedrich Schult, *Das plastische Werk* (1960) and *Das graphische Werk* (1958) have appeared in Hamburg; the third volume, to deal with Barlach's drawings, is still in preparation. Barlach's poetic work appeared in Munich (1958–1959) in three volumes: *Die Dramen; Die Prosa I; Die Prosa II*. A major portion of Barlach's extant letters is included in *Ernst Barlach: Leben und Werk in seinen Briefen*, edited by Friedrich Dross (Munich, 1952). Major selections from his plastic works and drawings, as photographed by Friedrich Hewicker, were edited by Wolf Stubbe (*Plastik*, Munich, 1959; *Zeichnungen*, Munich, 1961). Excerpts from Barlach's letters have appeared in the translation by M. E. Knight in the anthology *Art and Artist* (Berkeley and Los Angeles, 1956). Excerpts from Barlach's letters, diaries and other writings appeared in translation by Naomi Jackson Groves in *The Transformations of God* (Hamburg, 1962). *Three Plays by Ernst Barlach* was published in Minneapolis in 1964. It contains *The Flood, The Genuine Sedemunds*, and *The Blue Boll*: the translations are by Alex Page.

The author has consulted essays by Sheldon Cheney, Edson M. Chick, Naomi Jackson Groves, Manfred L. Keiler and other scholars, that appeared in American magazines, and the vast number of articles he found in German newspapers and periodicals, especially writings by such experts as Hanns Theodor Flemming, Walther Huder, Gottfried Sello, Hugo Sieker, Wolf Stubbe, and Martin Urban. For advice and help, he is indebted to the officers and staff of the Ernst Barlach Gesellschaft, the Barlach-Haùs and the Staatliche Landesbildstelle, all in Hamburg, and to Inter Nationes, Bonn.

Since the end of the war, Barlach exhibitions in his native country have been so numerous that only a few major ones will be listed below.

October 1948	Memorial Exhibition at the Kunsthalle, Hamburg: The Collection of Hermann F. Reemtsma
December 1951 to February 1952	German Academy of Arts, Berlin
July–August 1958	Kunsthalle, Hamburg: Collected Graphic Work

January to March 1959   Kunsthalle, Bremen

August to October 1959   Staedtische Galerie und Lenbach-Galerie, Munich: Sculpture, Drawings, Graphic Work

In the fall of 1963, numerous galleries and museums in West Germany celebrated the twenty-fifth anniversary of Barlach's death with special exhibitions. In 1965, the Kunsthalle, Hamburg, showed drawings from the artist's estate at Guestrow.

In England, the only major Barlach exhibition was to be seen at the Arts Council, London, in 1961.

In the United States the country's first major Barlach show, at the University of Nebraska Art Galleries, Lincoln, Nebraska, opened in October 1955. The show was subsequently seen at Seattle, Dayton, and Cambridge. Sculptures and drawings by Barlach were shown in New York at Borgenicht Galleries in 1956 and the St. Etienne Galleries in 1962. In 1962–1963 a loan exhibition of sculpture, drawings and prints, organized by Hamburg's Barlach Society, was circulated in ten American cities by the Smithsonian Institution.